CREATE

ONE-YEAR BLOG &
EDITORIAL PLANNER

CREATE

One-Year Blog & Editorial Planner

MEERA KOTHAND

www.meerakothand.com

Copyright © 2021

While the publisher and author have used their best
efforts in preparing this guide and planner, they make no
representations or warranties with respect to the accuracy
or completeness of the contents of this document. The
information is to be used at your own risk. Every situation
is different and will not be an exact replica of the examples
given in this e-book. The author cannot guarantee results
or any specific outcomes gleaned from using the methods
outlined in the following pages.

PERMISSIONS

You have permission to photograph this planner for your
review and include any photographs or videos in your
social media sharing. Please do not photograph and/or
film the whole planner.

For other permission requests, please email the author:
meera@meerakothand.com

First edition published 2017. Second edition 2021.

CREATE

ONE-YEAR BLOG & EDITORIAL PLANNER

CREATE EXCEPTIONAL CONTENT,
GET MORE DONE, AND SMASH THROUGH
YOUR BUSINESS GOALS

Second Edition

MEERA KOTHAND

CONTENTS

MAKE SURE YOU VISUALIZE WHAT YOU REALLY WANT, NOT WHAT SOMEONE ELSE WANTS FOR YOU

JERRY GILLIES, AUTHOR

INTRODUCTION

Two questions I'm asked pretty often:

Is it supposed to be this hard? Or am I doing it all wrong?

If you feel like you're losing control of your business or blog, feeling overwhelmed or just plain lost—whether you're just starting out or you're further along—I'm sure you've asked yourself these questions.

Navigating everything you need to do and know to build a blog and business is challenging and overwhelming.

Email marketing, writing blog posts, social media promotion, growing your traffic and an audience—there are so many moving pieces, and bringing it all together can seem like an impossible task.

There is no magic bullet, secret formula, or quick fix as some people would like you to believe. You don't earn six figures a year working merely two hours a day and get there in just one month.

Yes, *it is* hard and the learning curve is ridiculously steep, especially when you're starting out. It doesn't help that everyone else seems to be on every single social media platform out there.

They're doing YouTube because, hey, you can't go wrong with video! They're posting on Instagram thrice a day because the last podcast they listened to said that it was *the* platform to be on. They're publishing one blog post a day because it apparently gets you more traffic.

These statements aren't necessarily wrong.

Content *is* important and *still* extremely effective. Every month, 329 million people read blogs, and businesses that blog 15 plus times per month get 5 times more traffic than their peers.[1] Those who are actively creating content see 67% more digital leads than those who don't.[2]

But are you attracting the *right* leads? Does your content contribute to growth? Do you see results from it?

The business owners and bloggers who have the most success create **purposeful and intentional content.** They don't jump from one shiny object to the next.

They're clear on what they need to do to achieve their most immediate milestone. They also know what to focus on. You don't want the "busyness" of creating content to consume you and impede your growth.

That's the reason I created this planner.

CREATE is a planning and editorial system designed specifically to help ambitious bloggers and solopreneurs like you create intentional content. It combines everything I've learned from working with clients and students as well as how I plan my own year—meshing content with strategy and purpose.

When I launched the first version of this planner back in 2017, I did so because I saw a huge gap in how small business owners and solopreneurs dealt with content. Content was something you churned out regularly for traffic.

Because it was the right thing to do.

Because everyone was doing it.

But it was *never* something that aligned with your business goals; *never* something that made your ideal readers crave your products and services; *never* something that positioned you as an expert.

The blog planners in the market also focused purely on vanity metrics—page views and followers. Never on the stats that mattered.

The goal of the CREATE planner was to change all of that. As I write this, over 7,000 business owners have since gone through the planner and have incorporated the CREATE system into their businesses.

THE CREATE SYSTEM

At the crux of the CREATE System is the 5-Step Planning Process. This process has been significant to my business growth. If you're familiar with my work, this is a process that I keep coming back to over and over again in my books.

I'll walk you through each of the steps in detail over the next few pages.

If you're new to my work and new to any type of content planning, several of the terms and concepts I'm going to introduce to you may seem alien.

They may take time to understand.

It may seem like an incredible amount of prep work when you just want to jump in and start filling out these pages. But stay with me and trust in the process.

Remember that this isn't just a planner. **It's a business system.**

It may take time for you to internalize it. To know how to apply it to your own offers. To get familiar with the terms.

I want to assure you that this is normal. I still refer back to these frameworks time and time again when I'm planning my own content.

HOW THE CREATE PLANNER IS STRUCTURED

You start with an overview of your entire plan for the year. The emphasis is on breaking your year down into campaigns and promotions.

You also have pages for each month where you work on content, email, and detailed tasks. If you prefer an overview of the month in a two-page calendar, you have that too. The order of how you fill these in depends on how you like to plan.

I like to see an overview of the month by plotting key dates into the monthly calendar. These key dates are what I'm launching for the month as well as affiliate and sales promotions. I then work backward and flesh out the details—content, emails, and other tasks. This helps me reverse engineer what I need to do to reach my goals.

You may decide to flesh out the content and details first before filling these into the monthly overview.

It's YOUR planner and YOU decide how you want to use it.

The point of mapping out both the overview and details is to ensure that your goals and content are aligned with one other. It helps you work smarter so that you don't ever create content and send emails simply to fill your publishing schedule.

For instance, if you're launching a course this month on intentional eating, your content for this month as well as the one prior to that needs to be centered around intentional eating.

It needs to focus on bringing attention to the problem your course is trying to solve, instill desire for your solution, and let the reader know why they needs to take action to solve the problem and how *your offer* would be the perfect solution.

Do you see how this creates purposeful content?

The structure of this editorial planner will constantly remind you to create content around your goals. You'll also have the right questions in front of you to help you understand your audience better and to create content designed to showcase your products and services.

You'll chart a content and email strategy that gels with your business and blogging goals. You'll have a predictable business calendar. Every decision you make will be calculated and intentional.

Note: The planner is undated, so you can start using it at any time of the year. YOUR CREATE SPACES are blank pockets within the planner for you to brainstorm and jot down your ideas. YOUR SWIPE STASH are blank pockets within the planner to swipe good ideas and headlines you've seen others use and that you can tweak for your own use. YOUR EMAIL SWIPE STASH are blank pockets within the planner to swipe good email ideas and subject lines you've seen others use and that you can tweak for your own use.

WHAT'S NEW IN THIS VERSION

When CREATE was first published in 2017, most CREATE users were beginners. Over the years, with more CREATE users surpassing their business goals and adding multiple products and services to their business, I wanted to create a space where they could plan their campaigns and promotions. That's the reason I added the following:

• Content One-Sheet

• Email One-Sheet

• CEO / Vision Space

• Campaign One-Sheet

• Campaign Analysis

These are (as the name suggests) single pages that provide an overview of strategy and relevant details. There's also greater guidance on creating content around your products and services. I'll walk you through what these are over the next few pages.

THIS PLANNER IS FOR YOU IF...

You're creating a business around your blog or if your blog supports your existing business. If your main content channel is a podcast or video, can you still use this planner? Absolutely!

It's for you if you want to hold yourself accountable, track your progress, and make major strides in your blog and business.

It's for you if you're done being ambushed by shiny object syndrome, procrastination, and overcommitment.

And if you're here, you definitely are!

By using this blog and editorial planner, you will accomplish more, feel a greater sense of satisfaction, and actually make progress toward your larger vision for your blog.

If you have ever felt anxious staring at a blank planner full of pages, CREATE will hold your hand through the process. You will get prompts and tips so that you're never lost as to how to plan your months and quarters.

You'll be amazed at how far you will have come in a year if you start taking action today.

LET'S GO!

DOWNLOAD YOUR BONUS PACK

Before we dive in, go to

CREATEPLANNER.COM/PLANNER-BONUS/

to download the guided videos and resources that go together with this book.

GUIDED VIDEO SERIES:
HOW TO USE
THE CREATE
— BLOG & —
EDITORIAL
PLANNER

• BONUS MASTERCLASS •
HOW TO
CREATE CONTENT
THAT SUPPORTS (NOT SABOTAGES)
YOUR BUSINESS

4 (+1) TIME
BUCKET IDEAS
SWIPE FILE

IT'S FOR YOU IF YOU WANT TO HOLD YOURSELF ACCOUNTABLE, TRACK YOUR PROGRESS, AND MAKE MAJOR STRIDES IN YOUR BLOG AND BUSINESS.

START
HERE

CONCEPTS INTRODUCED IN THE CREATE SYSTEM

THE 5-STEP PLANNING PROCESS

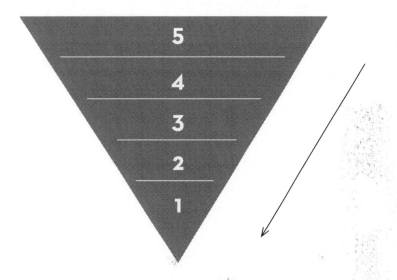

1. Determine your stage of growth & stage milestones.

2. Lay out your goals for the year and quarter (each goal helps you inch toward achieving your stage milestones).

3. Break your year into campaigns/promotions/themes.

4. Determine content and marketing assets that would support the goal of each month's campaign/promotion/theme.

5. Bring these together in a calendar & workflow.

Before we go into the process, let's have a look at the different stages so you can determine where you are.

STAGE IDENTIFICATION

There is so much to do when it comes to running an online business. You can never ever be "done." It's easy to be thrown off course by looking at the magnitude of work in front of you.

How then do you manage this?

Focus only on activities that are crucial for the stage that your business is at. Aim for hitting only your stage-appropriate milestones. Anything that doesn't fit in with your stage of growth is not important—at least for now. That's the best way to prevent overwhelm from sabotaging you and your blog. That's how I survived!

When you identify where you're at and where you need to go, you can create a plan for everything you need to do to reach your milestone.

The table below gives an overview of the different stages of building your online platform and their respective milestones. I've also included revenue streams that pair perfectly with your stage of growth. Look out for pitfalls like launching memberships and premium courses as your first digital products. I dive into this further in my book *Selling the Intangible*. You can have a look at it at readmeera.com/intangible.

Ultimately you want to **stack your wins.** Building a business is a marathon. Not a sprint.

	STAGES					
	STARTUP STAGE		**GROWTH STAGE**		**SCALE STAGE**	
	0	**1**	**2**	**3**	**4**	**5**
MILE-STONE	Launch your biz with a solid foundation. Establish minimal viable plans.	Nurture & grow your list to 500–1,000 subscribers.	Earn your first $1K / Create and launch your first product or service.	Earn a full-time income. Expand revenue streams and sell products via evergreen funnels.	Expand revenue streams. Outsource noncore projects or tasks.	Automate selling of core or signature products. Put in place more systems. Incorporate paid ads into core strategy.
TEAM	Just You	Just You	Just You	You + Contract Help	You + Contract Help	You + Contract Help + Small Team
HURDLE	Steep learning curve. Lack of clarity. Shiny object syndrome.	Working at getting a consistent number of subscribers every day. Converting traffic to subscribers. Business costs when you're making nothing much/anything as yet.	Learning how to sell or launch. Feast-or-famine cycle.	Getting over resistance and blocks in investing. Learning how to sell effectively.		Balancing business expenses with need to grow your business further. Shifting into a CEO role. Knowing how to streamline and simplify for better results.
REVENUE	$0–$1K		$1K–$3K	$3K–$5K	$5K–$10K	$10–$30K
REVENUE STREAMS	Coaching Offering a Service Affiliate Marketing	Tripwire/Tiny Products	Signature or Specialist Courses Hybrid (Group Coaching + Courses)	Membership Subscription Box Mastermind Speaking Agency		

A PRIMER FOR SETTING GOALS

Before you set any goal, ask yourself the following questions:

- **Does it fit in with your stage of growth?**

Every goal you set and every task you do should focus on reaching that milestone. Everything that doesn't fit should be thrown out.

Likewise, if you're a course junkie and want to know when to invest in a course, check back in with your blogging stage. Anything that doesn't move the needle for you at this blogging stage is not a priority. Want to sign up for a webinar? Ask yourself if this will help you reach your end-point milestone for the stage you're in.

If it does, sign up for it.

If it doesn't, don't.

- **Is this a vanity metric or can it be broken down into growth actions and tasks you can directly influence? Is it possible to have a time or date stamp on each of these growth actions and tasks?**

What growth actions can you directly influence? Don't fall into the trap of vanity metrics. For instance, have a look at this:

QUARTER 1 GOALS

1. Increase email list to 500 subscribers

2. Make first $200–$500

You can't influence these directly. But here's what you can influence:

ACTIONS BASED ON GOAL 1

- I will make an additional opt-in incentive.

- I will guest post on four blogs by the end of the quarter.

- I will run one promoted pin campaign.

ACTIONS BASED ON GOAL 2

- I will write two detailed tutorials on my chosen affiliate product.

- I will update the affiliate links in my old posts.

- I will make a bonus e-book for subscribers who purchase through my affiliate link.

See the difference?

When you break down your goals in this way and focus on growth actions you can directly influence, your goal immediately becomes attainable because you know exactly how you're going to get there.

> **Note:** I recommend picking only 2–3 goals per quarter. To see results you will need at least a solid quarter to work through these goals.

PLAN YOUR YEAR USING CAMPAIGNS

This is where the magic happens!

Learning to structure my year in terms of campaigns was one of my biggest aha moments in business.

Because once you learn how to do this, it's easy to get focused.

It gives you a big picture view of your year. It helps you to align your calendar as closely as possible with your marketing goals. It also reduces the number of decisions you need to make and helps with consistency.

A campaign or promotion is nothing more than **a coordinated set of content pieces** that you create and distribute over a fixed time frame to achieve a specific goal. These pieces could also be focused around a theme. Every single piece of content you put out during this time frame is focused on advancing that goal.

This is similar to how most publishing sites structure their content. They have editorial calendars that go with a monthly theme, and they organize their content based on that. For instance, August is back to school, January is about new year resolutions and goals, February is about relationships.

When you create content in this way, you take your readers through a journey over the length of your campaign (which runs over a specific time period). It nudges your reader toward the end goal of the campaign. On pages 79 and 80 of the planner, you will plan your campaigns/themes for the year.

5 MAIN CAMPAIGN TYPES

	OFFER	Discount, Trial, Flash Sale, Limited Offer, Limited Quantities, Xmas & Black Friday
	EVENT	Summit, Webinar, Workshop Challenge, Video Series
	CONTENT	VIP List, Authority / Visibility Building, Early Bird
	SEASONAL	Business-Related Holidays, Veterans Day
	BUZZ BUILDING	Giveaways, Contests

EXAMPLES OF CAMPAIGNS

- *Authority Building*

  A campaign designed to raise awareness about your brand and share your expertise in a topic you want to be known for.

- *VIP*

  A campaign designed to attract an interest list for your products and services.

- *Affiliate Promotion*

  A campaign designed to build interest and get buy-in for a program or tool you're an affiliate of.

- *Launch*

  The most common type. This is a campaign designed to build interest and get buy-in for your products and services.

Once you have a theme/campaign, determine your goal:

- Do you need to prime your audience for a launch of an offer?

- Are you trying to help break assumptions or false beliefs they may have about a topic?

- Is there a viewpoint you'd like to share?

- Are you teaching them something?

Based on your campaign/theme, you'll be able to determine what you need to spend your time on for that month and what marketing assets and content you need to create. All of this will go into your **CAMPAIGN ONE-SHEET.**

END GOAL	WHAT YOUR CONTENT SHOULD ENCAPSULATE
BUILD AUTHORITY & KNOW-LIKE-TRUST	• How you can help them solve their problems related to the topic of your niche • Why they should trust you • What you can offer them that's different
SELL OFFER	• Bring attention to the problem your offer solves • Instill desire for the offer • Remove your subscribers' objections

How do you decide what content will *feed* this campaign?

We'll look at content strategy over the next few pages. This will give you a solid foundation as to how to pick and create the right content pieces for each campaign.

CONTENT STRATEGY

When done right, a content strategy will help you create content that

1. supports your business's core mission and goals,

2. attracts and serves your target audience,

3. sells your products and services for you.

This is what purposeful content does. Content that's created in a vacuum is wasted content.

Whether you're creating a blog post, email series, or email course, you need to have a clear reason as to why you're doing so. You need to define the purpose and goal of that content even before you create it.

How exactly do I define content?

Content includes all of the following:

- email
- social media posts
- content channels (YouTube, microblogging, blog posts, podcasts, etc.)
- infographics
- videos
- and more

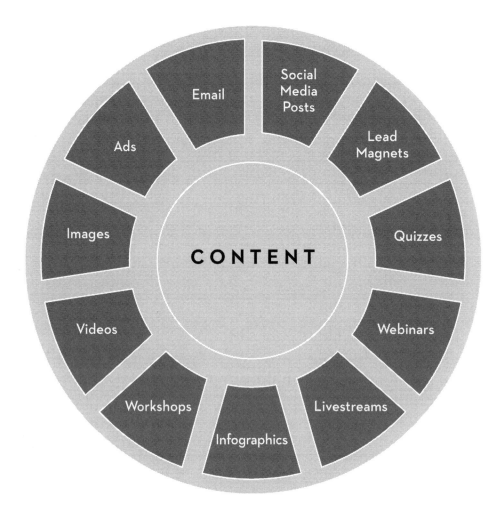

At the heart of creating purposeful content and planning your content strategy, lies a clear understanding of your business and the products and services you're offering.

If you're familiar with my content and you're familiar with the concept of breaking your content into categories, then go ahead and *skip this section.*

Note: Even if you have done the exercises before, take stock of where your content is right now and where you want it to be. Does it still serve your business? Are there categories that you can get rid of because your business has shifted? Do you need to shift your content focus because of a new business direction? Consider these questions as you attempt this exercise again. A fresh pair of eyes is what every blog and business needs.

How are you going to help your ideal reader?

This is where your **value proposition** has to come in.

It forms the basis for every single piece of content you create. How can you come up with an all-encompassing purpose or value proposition for your blog?

First, answer these three questions:

1. What group do you want to help, i.e., who is your ideal reader?

2. What are they struggling with that your business could help them with?

For example, let's say you want to help women. The topic you want to help them with is starting a home business.

Now you have two areas to work with. Break this down further. Try to get specific with your answers. You're not helping just any women, but single moms. And not just any type of home business, but a virtual assistant (VA) business.

Once you break it down in this way, your content angle takes on a very different dimension. Content for a single mom with two kids trying to run a home-based VA business is very different from content for a twentysomething just out of college trying to run a home-based VA business.

Then plot your answers into one of these two statements. Do this exercise for your blog right now.

I educate/inspire/entertain/teach/help _____
who want to _____ .

I show _____ how _____ .

Examples:

• I help authors learn how to market themselves and sell more books.

• I inspire twentysomethings to travel the world on a shoestring budget.

• I show food bloggers how easy it is to take their own pictures and edit them.

3. What content or topic do you want to be known for?

Let's not get into the generalist or specialist argument here. There are various opinions. But don't you agree that you are more attractive to an ideal reader who needs help for a specific problem if you know your topic in-depth versus if you are a jack-of-all-trades?

Think about 1-2 topics you want to be known for.

Struggling with this? A **YES** on all of the questions below means that you have a winner.

• You can see yourself building offers around these topics.

• You have enough interest in this topic that you can see yourself discussing it for the next 3-5 years at least.

• You are excited to keep up to date with the trends of this topic.

I'm going to encourage you to limit your choices to just two topics for now.

Now that you're clear about how you're helping your audience and what you want to be known for, let's dive deeper!

What content categories will support this purpose?

You know the end point. You know how you're going to help your reader. But your content has to lead them there. Each category supports your overall purpose. And within each category, you have sub-categories and topics.

Now, list out the content categories that will support your business's purpose. You don't have to fill in all five categories. Three categories will be perfect to start with. It would be better to go narrow and deep with your content than wide and shallow.

Let's move on to your sub-categories. To figure out your sub-categories, ask yourself what your reader needs to know to become well-versed in the category. Likewise, when you're fleshing out blog posts for each sub-category, ask yourself what the reader needs to know to become well-versed in the sub-category.

Let's take a website for new authors. The categories could be

- Marketing your author brand & books

- Hone your writing craft

- Getting published

Let's break it down into Category > Sub-Category > Content Pieces.

CATEGORY – MARKETING YOUR AUTHOR BRAND & BOOKS

 Ask yourself: What does the reader need to know to become an expert or to become proficient in this category?

Here are two possible sub-categories:

1. How to build your author platform

2. How to get your books noticed

Let's break each of these sub-categories down.

SUB-CATEGORY 1: HOW TO BUILD YOUR AUTHOR PLATFORM

 Ask yourself: What does the reader need to know to become an expert or to become proficient in this sub-category?

Content Pieces:

5 essential components of an author website

10 types of reviews publishers look for on an author website

SUB-CATEGORY 2: HOW TO GET YOUR BOOKS NOTICED

 Ask yourself: What does the reader need to know to become an expert or to become proficient in this sub-category?

Content Pieces:

How to write a standout book description

15 essential elements that make a killer book cover

You can expand and dive deeper into each of your categories and sub-categories. This system will give you an endless list of blog post ideas to work with at any one time.

You've just made the task of creating topics at least 50% easier with this system. **If you have no products or services as yet, this is the system you want to use to map out your content.**

But what if you do have products and services. Then, the next system would be apt for you!

PLANNING CONTENT AROUND YOUR PRODUCTS AND SERVICES

Have you noticed that some of your readers buy more quickly from you compared to others?

Ever wondered why, even though they may have been exposed to the same type of content for the same period of time or perhaps are even brand new to you and your brand?

It's most likely because readers have different states of awareness. They're at different stages in their journey. Have a look at the diagram below.

If you're familiar with my content, you know that I'm a huge fan of the five states of awareness created by copywriting legend Eugene Schwartz.

This states that a prospective buyer, reader, or subscriber starts by being problem unaware, then becomes problem aware, solution unaware, solution aware, and finally, most aware.

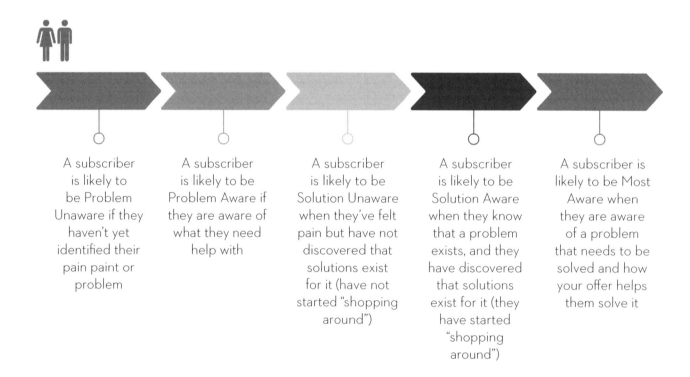

A subscriber is likely to be Problem Unaware if they haven't yet identified their pain paint or problem

A subscriber is likely to be Problem Aware if they are aware of what they need help with

A subscriber is likely to be Solution Unaware when they've felt pain but have not discovered that solutions exist for it (have not started "shopping around")

A subscriber is likely to be Solution Aware when they know that a problem exists, and they have discovered that solutions exist for it (they have started "shopping around")

A subscriber is likely to be Most Aware when they are aware of a problem that needs to be solved and how your offer helps them solve it

Other concepts drop the reader (listener or viewer) into broader phases such as Awareness – Consideration – Decision, or into broad descriptions of Beginner – Intermediate – Advanced.

The terms may vary, but the groupings largely overlap with one another. What's more important is that you understand that the content they need and the questions they have at each of these stages will differ.

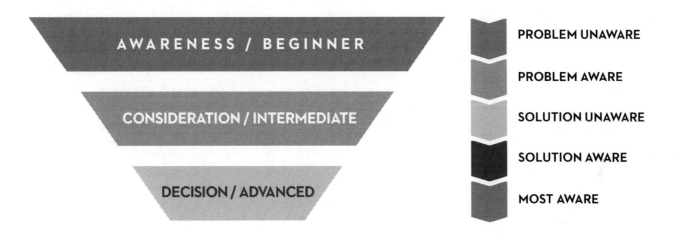

Every offer you have solves a problem for your ideal buyer. But why would they buy if they have no clue they need something to be solved in the first place? I've talked about this in my books *The One Hour Content Plan* and *The Profitable Content System*.

What does the reader need to be aware of before they are ready to purchase your products or engage your services? They need to be aware of the problem your product is solving. Why it needs to be solved. How much better their lives would be and the benefits of solving the problem. Finally, they need to know how your product or service fits into the puzzle.

But you'll get readers who are at different ends of the spectrum. Some may have no clue about the problem you are solving. Some may be actively searching for a solution to it and comparing different products and services in the market.

Different content pieces will appeal to these different readers depending on where they are in the buying process.

What questions do they usually have before saying yes to your offer? Here's how you can break content ideas down based on their journey.

AWARENESS/BEGINNER

The content here is likely to be centered around the **WHAT** and **WHY**. They have identified a symptom of a potential problem. They may not have identified the real problem but rather are looking for ways to soothe or get rid of their symptoms.

They may also be embarrassed by the questions they have due to their lack of knowledge on this topic.

Create content that shows them everything they could be doing wrong. It should also bring attention to the problem at hand, so get them to sit up and take notice.

• Why should I use [TOPIC] in my life/business?

• What is [TOPIC] about?

• What's the meaning of [BASIC TERMS/WORDS/JARGON SURROUNDING THE TOPIC]?

• Why should I stop [DOING SOMETHING RELATED TO THE TOPIC]?

• What [MISTAKES RELATED TO THE TOPIC] should I stop making?

CONSIDERATION/INTERMEDIATE

The content here is likely to be centered around **HOW (application or implementation).**

They have clearly identified their problem and are actively looking for solutions to solve their pain points. You have their attention and you want to throw them a lifeline. How can they solve these pain points or problems?

• How do I do [ONE ASPECT OF THE TOPIC]?

• What tools should I use for [ONE ELEMENT OF THE TOPIC]?

• How can I implement [TOPIC] to do [ONE ASPECT OF THE PROCESS]?

DECISION/ADVANCED

At the **Decision** stage, your reader has a clear understanding of the problem as well as how your solution, framework, or method can fit their needs, their life, or their business. These are the readers who are most primed and ready to buy.

- How can I get more of [DESIRED RESULT]?

- What do I need to do to get [DESIRED RESULT]?

- What am I missing out on to get [DESIRED RESULT]?

What you want to do is list 5–10 questions your audience has at each stage for each offer you have.

Here's an example of what the STAGE X 10 Framework looks like. **If you *have* products and services, *this* is the system you want to use to plot out your content.**

STAGE X 10 FRAMEWORK

WHY-WHAT Awareness / Beginner Stage / Bring attention to the problem	
HOW Consideration / Intermediate Stage / Bring interest in the solution	
DESIRE Decision / Advanced Stage / Bring desire for your solution	

CASE STUDY – Visibility & PR

Joan helps female entrepreneurs grow their businesses through strategic public relations.

OFFER: She offers an in-depth DIY course for small business owners who want to start getting noticed through strategic PR.

CORE PROBLEM & SOLUTION: Several business owners neglect PR completely because they don't think it's a necessary part of their strategy. A PR team is also expensive, and they don't think a DIY solution is viable. Joan offers a perfect starter solution and takes someone from nothing to crafting a strategic PR plan for their business even if they don't have a lot of time, are starting from scratch, or have failed at PR before.

WHAT DO THEY NEED TO KNOW BEFORE BEING READY TO BUY: Her ideal customer needs to be aware that PR is a crucial strategy not just for business owners further along in the journey but also for those in the beginner phase as well. They also need to be convinced that a DIY PR solution is a viable option and one that can be successful.

WHY-WHAT — Awareness / Beginner Stage / Bring attention to the problem	Why PR should be a part of your strategy even if your business is brand new
	7 reasons why you should care about PR even if you're a one-woman shop
	Stop looking like an amateur! Top 10 PR blunders small businesses make and what to learn from them
HOW — Consideration / Intermediate Stage / Bring interest in the solution	The beginner's guide to using PR for your small business
	How to figure out what topics to pitch yourself for
	5 PR tools every entrepreneur needs
	6 do-it-yourself PR tips for small businesses
	4 easy ways to get publicity for your business
DESIRE — Decision / Advanced Stage / Bring desire for your solution	DIY PR: 10 public relations solutions for small business owners
	Here's how to use PR to attract more clients and boost sales

Want to explore these ideas further? Check out *The Profitable Content System* at readmeera.com/profitablecontent.

YOUR CREATE SPACE

FLESH OUT YOUR SUB-CATEGORIES
AND CONTENT PIECES

FLESH OUT YOUR SUB-CATEGORIES
AND CONTENT PIECES

YOUR CREATE SPACE

FLESH OUT THE STAGE ×10 FRAMEWORK FOR EACH OFFER YOU HAVE OVER THE NEXT FEW PAGES

Name of Offer	Social Media Calendar

What core problem does the offer solve?	**WHY-WHAT** Awareness / Beginner Stage / Bring attention to the problem	
What does someone need to know before being ready to buy?	**HOW** Consideration / Intermediate Stage / Bring interest in the solution	
	DESIRE Decision / Advanced Stage / Bring desire for your solution	

Name of Offer	Content Runway Q1 2022

What core problem does the offer solve?	WHY-WHAT Awareness / Beginner Stage / Bring attention to the problem	why they need to use a strategic content strategy on their business what is content why they should stop creating random content
simple ways to create a plan content that grows their Business		

What does someone need to know before being ready to buy?	HOW Consideration / Intermediate Stage / Bring interest in the solution	
	DESIRE Decision / Advanced Stage / Bring desire for your solution	

| Name of Offer | List Building Runway- Q1 2022 |

| What core problem does the offer solve? | **WHY-WHAT** Awareness / Beginner Stage / Bring attention to the problem | |

| What does someone need to know before being ready to buy? | **HOW** Consideration / Intermediate Stage / Bring interest in the solution | |

| | **DESIRE** Decision / Advanced Stage / Bring desire for your solution | |

Name of Offer	Beginner Q2- 2022

What core problem does the offer solve?	**WHY-WHAT** Awareness / Beginner Stage / Bring attention to the problem	
	HOW Consideration / Intermediate Stage / Bring interest in the solution	
What does someone need to know before being ready to buy?	**DESIRE** Decision / Advanced Stage / Bring desire for your solution	

Name of Offer	Course Creation Q3 2022

| What core problem does the offer solve? | **WHY-WHAT** Awareness / Beginner Stage / Bring attention to the problem | |

| What does someone need to know before being ready to buy? | **HOW** Consideration / Intermediate Stage / Bring interest in the solution | |

| | **DESIRE** Decision / Advanced Stage / Bring desire for your solution | |

YOUR SWIPE STASH

A swipe stash/file is a collection of templates and examples that have worked for someone else that you "swipe" for your own inspiration.

That's what I did when I started out. I swiped headlines and subject lines I liked—landing pages and sales pages that spoke to me. I learned from the structure they used. I took that structure and then made it my own by adding my unique take and spin on it.

You're basically starting with something that you know works, rather than from scratch. You can learn a lot from your swipe stash, and it'll save you a whole lot of stress by having something to lean on.

This is your swipe stash section to clip headlines or topics you've seen others use—that you can contribute a different take on or add to the existing literature. There is a section for EMAIL SWIPE STASH ideas as well later in the planner.

YOUR SWIPE STASH

REPURPOSING CONTENT

Repurposing content is maximizing the reach of a piece of content through different formats and different channels.

This isn't just sharing the same piece of content on a different channel.

Sure, doing this extends the reach of that piece of content. But repurposing is **offering your existing piece of content in a different format.**

So if your content is primarily text-based, you're changing it to audio, video, or images. If your content is primarily video-based, you're changing it to text, audio, or images.

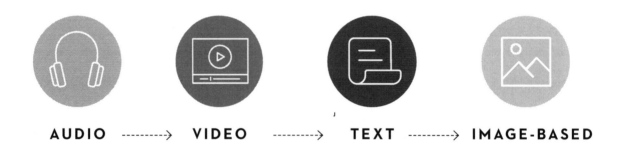

AUDIO --------> **VIDEO** --------> **TEXT** --------> **IMAGE-BASED**

How can you incorporate a repurposing strategy into the day-to-day of how you do things?

Because if you don't, it will never become a part of your process.

This is what I call **Minimum Viable Repurposing.**

Here are some questions for you to consider.

1. What is your main content format?

If it's a YouTube channel, your primary format is video. So your repurposing options would fall under the other three content formats: audio, text, and image-based formats.

Likewise, if your primary content format is a podcast (hence audio), you have video, text, and image-based formats to work with.

2. What alternative traffic channels are you active on?

These are not your primary traffic channels but others where you are active or relatively active on. This alternative traffic channel is a platform your audience is active on as well, and it should have given you some results in terms of engagement, reach, or lead generation.

My primary traffic channel is Pinterest. Alternative channels that don't get me as much organic reach, but that I'm familiar with and have received decent engagement from my audience, are Facebook and Instagram.

3. What other content formats do you like to create?

I mentioned in my book *The One Hour Content Plan* that I don't believe you have to create content in a particular format because everyone says you should or because it gives you a great return on investment.

So if you're going to lock yourself in a room crying at the thought of doing videos or writing a blog post for that matter, I'll say rethink that format again. Lean in to those that come naturally to you and you'll look at content with enthusiasm—not disdain.

Note: If you don't have the bandwidth to repurpose content, you have my absolute permission to skip it! There's always a give and take, and I didn't start repurposing my content till a good number of years into my business.

DIFFERENTIATE YOUR CONTENT CHANNELS

Before we head into email strategy, let's address a common question.

How do you know what content to post on what platform without sounding like you're saying the same thing everywhere?

Any content that you share on any content channel is likely to fall into one of these five main groups.

---

5 CONTENT GROUPS

EDUCATION   **CONVERSATION**   **INSPIRATION**   **ENTERTAINMENT**   **CONNECTION**

Let's take a look at education.

When you educate your audience, you bring awareness to their pain points and problems.

You also raise interest and generate desire for your products and services.

But it's not just that.

You also build trust and authority with this category of content.

This is very likely the grouping that is used to generate traffic back to your site or to help you turn readers/listeners/viewers into subscribers. It's responsible for building your email list.

The primary grouping for my blog is education.

What comes under education? Have a look at the diagram below.

EDUCATION ··

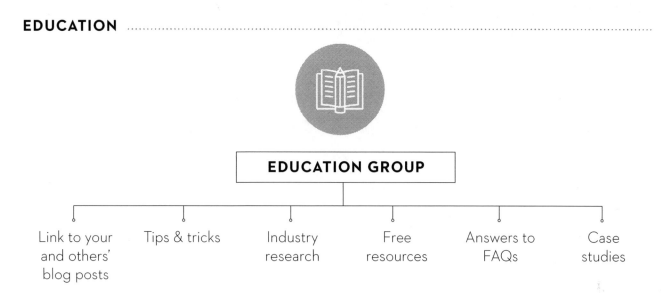

Conversation is the primary grouping for my email list.

A lot of content that I share by email has the content pieces outlined in the diagram below.

CONVERSATION ··

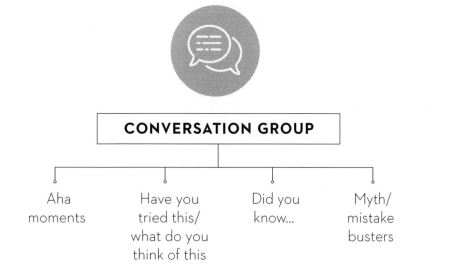

INSPIRATION ....

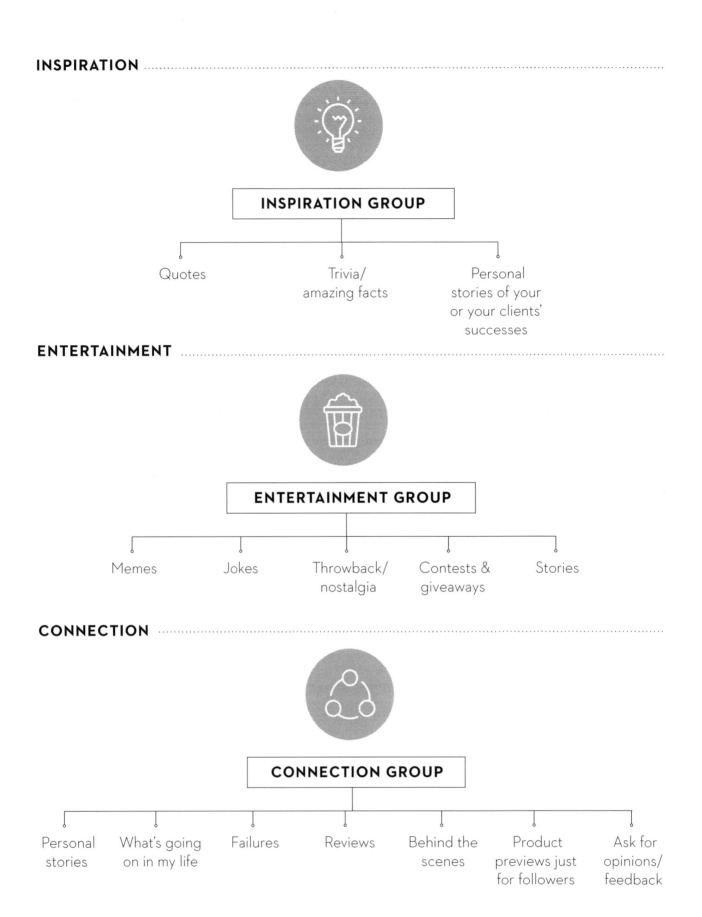

INSPIRATION GROUP

Quotes

Trivia/
amazing facts

Personal
stories of your
or your clients'
successes

ENTERTAINMENT ....

ENTERTAINMENT GROUP

Memes

Jokes

Throwback/
nostalgia

Contests &
giveaways

Stories

CONNECTION ....

CONNECTION GROUP

Personal
stories

What's going
on in my life

Failures

Reviews

Behind the
scenes

Product
previews just
for followers

Ask for
opinions/
feedback

Do you need all five groupings?

If you're starting with one main traffic platform and one main content channel (which you should), your content won't be able to cover all five groupings and that's ok!

The idea isn't to have content from all five groupings.

The idea is to have a simple process or framework to differentiate your content so you don't feel stumped or feel like you're saying the same thing.

CONTENT ONE-SHEET

What's your main content channel? For example, YouTube, podcast, etc.
(Note: I suggest starting with just ONE.)

P	S	WHAT ARE YOUR PRIMARY (P) AND SECONDARY (S) GROUPS FOR THIS CONTENT CHANNEL?
◯	◯	Conversation
◯	◯	Connection
◯	◯	Inspiration
◯	◯	Education
◯	◯	Entertainment

What's your main traffic channel? (Note: I suggest starting with just ONE.)

Main- pinterest
FB -
Instagram

Pick one content format you want to use for repurposing. (Skip if not applicable.)

Video- FB lives

Pick one alternative traffic platform you want to use for repurposing. (Skip if not Applicable.)

FB
Instagram

Identify 1-2 repurposing techniques. (Skip if not applicable.)

Example: Create a live video of the main points in your blog post. Make branded images for Instagram. Pick a point to talk about and link to your blog post.

AT THE HEART
OF CREATING
PURPOSEFUL
CONTENT AND
PLANNING
YOUR CONTENT
STRATEGY,
LIES A CLEAR
UNDERSTANDING
OF YOUR BUSINESS
AND THE PRODUCTS
AND SERVICES
YOU'RE OFFERING.

EMAIL STRATEGY

There's a lot of emphasis on your email list in this planner.

That's because you own your email list.

An email subscriber is more valuable than a social media follower.

Why?

Because if you had 1,000 followers, 1,000 organic visitors, and 1,000 email subscribers, and you tried to sell to all of them, you could expect to convert 6 followers, 25 visitors, and 42 subscribers (based on data from Monetate[3]). Email also gives the highest ROI of $44 for every dollar spent[4].

Email is critical in helping you support your business goals.

Email marketing is the use of emails to build a relationship with your customers and promote your products and services. But most businesses think of email marketing as just list growth even though list growth is only a small portion of your entire email marketing strategy. Email marketing is NOT list building alone.

There are several other critical aspects of email marketing.

THE 5-STEP ACTIVATION PROCESS

Have a look at the diagram below.

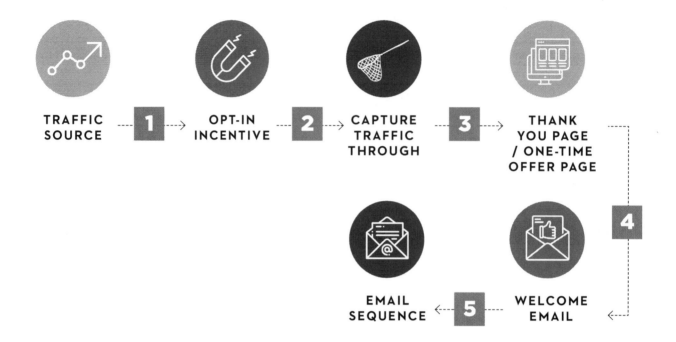

This is what I refer to as the **5-step activation process.**

You need all five parts if you want email marketing to work for your business.

How can things go wrong? In plenty of ways!

For starters, the wrong opt-in can bring you less-than-enthusiastic subscribers who do not buy…

Lack of clear instructions can skyrocket your unconfirmed subscriber numbers…

"Meh" landing pages and opt-in forms will let subscribers slip through the cracks even before they see your content…

So you want to make sure there are no gaps in this process.

This process helps you visualize your email marketing as a whole rather than as a bunch of random parts.

It gives you what you need to attract your ideal customers and take them from not knowing who you are to wanting to buy everything you put out for sale.

1. It starts with the traffic you send to your website or any page with an incentive or lead magnet (a free resource that you offer in exchange for an email address).

2. You then capture this traffic via a lead capture system such as an opt-in form or landing page.

3. You can then present your new subscriber with a one-time offer or tripwire. This is your first attempt at converting a subscriber into a buyer.

4. Your new subscriber receives your welcome email.

5. Depending on the end goal and pathway you've set out for that subscriber, you will send a dedicated series of emails or a follow-up email sequence that primes and nudges that subscriber toward that end goal.

You can have different traffic sources, different entry points for your subscribers (e.g., people subscribing via your messenger bot, Facebook page, or Instagram), or different offers you're trying to sell via your email sequence, but the basic flow stays the same.

Steps 1–5 are all you need to get started. You don't necessarily need a bot or to even do ads for that matter. It's these five steps alone that took my business full time and to six figures.

Take a moment now to think through the questions below. This will set a foundation for the type of emails you want to send and your intention for email marketing.

EMAIL ONE-SHEET

P	S	WHAT ARE YOUR PRIMARY (P) AND SECONDARY (S) GROUPS FOR EMAIL?
○	○	Conversation
○	○	Connection
○	○	Inspiration
○	○	Education
○	○	Entertainment

WHAT TYPE OF EMAILS DO YOU SEE YOURSELF SENDING?

Example: Curated newsletters, tips, stories, how-tos?

WHO ARE YOUR EMAIL SUPERSTARS? (PEOPLE YOU LOVE TO GET EMAILS FROM & WHY)

WHO	WHY

Now that you have a vision for how you want to approach your email list, let's formulate an email content strategy so you don't have to ever ask *"What do I send my list?"* The stress creeps in when you don't have even a cursory direction of what you're going to be writing in the first place.

The best way to curb this?

I highly recommend having overlapping themes for both email and your content strategy. Your email list has to complement your blog content and business goals. So it makes sense that they follow each other closely.

I use **email cues** such as the ones below to fill the spaces. Have a look at the diagram below.

• Tools

• Personal story

• Quick tip

• Shocking revelation

• Mistake

The combinations are endless. If planning your email content is something you've never done, you'll enjoy this exercise. This is part of a framework I teach in my course Profitable Email System.

	TOOL/ RESOURCE TIPS	YOUR MISTAKES/ FAILURES	BEHIND THE SCENES	INSPIRA-TIONAL	OUTSIDE STORY	MYTH	ANSWERS TO POPULAR QUESTIONS ON TOPIC
JAN: TOPIC Content	X		X	X		X	
FEB: TOPIC Content		X		X			
MAR: TOPIC		X		X	X		X
APR: TOPIC			X			X	
MAY: TOPIC	X		X				

TERMS USED IN THIS PLANNER

Content upgrades – A free resource or add-on content you offer with your blog post in exchange for your readers' email addresses.

Opt-in incentive – A free resource (e.g., cheat sheet, worksheet, guide, checklist) you offer in exchange for your readers' email addresses.

Cold subscribers – Subscribers who haven't opened or engaged with your emails in a certain period of time (usually 3–6 months).

Re-engagement campaign – This is a series of 2–3 emails you send your cold subscribers in an effort to discern their interest in staying on your list.

Clean your list – Every quarter, the planner prompts you to consider cleaning your list. A bigger list isn't necessarily better. For various reasons, many email subscribers stop opening and engaging with your emails after a certain period of time. You pay for every subscriber on your list, and it's good practice to re-engage these cold subscribers or delete them off your list.

Landing page – A distraction-free page with no navigation bar or external links that has a single goal of getting a reader to sign up to your opt-in form.

Conversion rate – How many people signed up on your opt-in form or landing page as a percentage of the total number of people who visited that opt-in form or landing page.

YOUR EMAIL SWIPE STASH

TIME BLOCKING WITH 4 (+1) TIME BUCKETS

In this section, I'll introduce you to 4 (+1) time buckets that categorize every single task that you will undertake for your business. These are

• Project

• Marketing

• Non-negotiable

• Web optimization/design

• CEO

Having four major time buckets to focus on will stop you from multitasking. If you think that your energy and resources are split 50/50 when you work on two different tasks, you're wrong. Switching between tasks sucks up time and energy because the brain has to recall instructions on how to do a previous task before getting into the swing of things.

Let me break each of these down, and I'll show you how they come together in a calendar.

 ### PROJECT BUCKET + "LOW-HANGING FRUIT" IDEAS

Projects are usually bigger tasks such as working on an info product, creating a new opt-in incentive, working on your email sequence, writing a sales page, setting up your membership site content, creating a media kit, working on a resource guide for your email list, or recording videos for a course. Projects give you a higher impact and return at the end. These are usually tasks that will benefit from a sprint.

A sprint is where you focus on just ONE activity for a short period of time so you can get more of it done.

A sprint may stretch for a week or more. It helps you focus on your project so you can ship it out fast.

LOW-HANGING FRUIT

I'm going to introduce you to a concept I always reference with my audience called Low-Hanging Fruit Ideas. These are the tiniest of things that can make the biggest impact. Every quarter, I'm going to encourage you to brainstorm a couple of these ideas. For instance, adding a second pricing tier to one of my checkout pages increased my revenue by 20%.

Here are a few other examples:

• Put in place a tripwire for your most trafficked category of content.

• List one question you get asked most often about your programs or offers. How can you answer that question on a visible space on your site or within your nurture sequence? Create a link that you can send people to.

• Review your open and click rates within an existing email sequence. Can you move up or remove emails that are underperforming?

I have a running list of ideas you can try. I have shared that list with you in the **BONUS** pack.

MARKETING OR PROMOTIONAL BUCKET

What is marketing?

Marketing isn't just about selling or promotion. It's also about attracting and capturing your ideal customers. In a nutshell, marketing is made up of these four activities:

ATTRACT ----→	**CAPTURE** ----→	**ENGAGE** ----→	**CONVERT**
Attract your ideal reader to your site.	Get them to sign up to your email list.	Engage with subscribers through emails. Establish trust.	Convert potential cutomers into actual customers. Convert customers into brand advocates by building a long-term relationship.

If no one knows that you or your business exists, it doesn't matter if you create exceptional content. This is why marketing and promoting your business is so important.

When I talk about marketing, I'm not just talking about scheduling your posts on social media or posting in Facebook groups. I'm talking about tasks that usually involve pitching your services to another party or getting in touch with someone to build a relationship. These tasks help to get your name and business out there.

Here are examples of marketing or promotional activities:

• Pitching a sponsored post

• Pitching a guest post

• Pitching a podcast

• Offering suggestions to influencers

• Offering to teach someone's audience for free

When I launched my site, I was pitching 2–3 guest posts every single week. The frequency and rigor with which you do this will depend heavily on your stage of business as well as your goals. If you have an upcoming book launch, this task may overshadow the others.

Likewise, if you're launching a new offer, you may want to work extensively on reaching new audiences to prepare for the launch of your offer.

 ## MAINTENANCE (OPTIMIZATION OR DESIGN) TASK BUCKET

This is another area that gets pushed to the bottom of the list unknowingly. There are always little things you can do to optimize your website.

I usually try to schedule one web optimization or design task per week.

This week, I might work on putting some testimonials and "as seen in" logos on some of my landing pages. Next week, I might refresh my resources page or about page. Do you need to add an exit intent pop-up? That's a web optimization task as well.

Here are a few other examples:

• Compress images using TinyPNG

• Optimize Pinterest descriptions

• Optimize landing pages and opt-in forms by adding logos and testimonials

I always have a running list of tasks that I can dip into each week. I have shared that list with you as well in the **BONUS** section. If I skip my schedule and don't do these for a while, I put all my design tasks together and do them as a major project that spans an entire week.

NON-NEGOTIABLE (OR BREAD AND BUTTER) TASK BUCKET

These are tasks that you have to do. They stay fixed on my schedule. I rarely move them around unless I absolutely have to. I keep them fixed because if I move them around, they don't get done. These tasks tend to be manual in nature, but they keep your business well-oiled and running smoothly.

Here are some examples:

• Scheduling social media posts

• Replying to subscriber emails

• Replying to blog post comments

• Replying to Twitter mentions

Don't let the names of the different tasks confuse you. This just gives you an order and structure to follow so that nothing falls through the cracks when you're growing your blog. When you're ready to outsource some of your work to an agency or a virtual assistant, non-negotiable and maintenance tasks are the first ones you can outsource. Being aware of what these are will make it easier for you to pass on these tasks.

THE (+1) CEO BUCKET

The (+1) Task Bucket is what I like to call the CEO or Vision Bucket. This is thirty minutes to an hour every week where you do nothing but let your ideas flow freely on what you could be creating for your business—possible business directions or ventures. You're not validating your ideas or judging the worth of those ideas. You're simply making a note of them. If you have sudden flashes of inspiration, those thoughts would go in here too. Whether you use this as a structured time for vision planning or keep this as a space to jot down your inspiration is completely up to you. But the more you "train" your mind to come up with new ideas, the easier it gets.

BRINGING THE 4 (+1) BUCKETS TOGETHER

Now that we've looked at the major blogging tasks, let me show you how they come together.

I use time blocking to structure my week. This is the easiest method and doesn't require me to learn a new technique. **The most important thing to do is identify your most productive time block.**

Be aware of when in the day you have the most energy as well. If you're on the move running errands or dropping off your kids and have to work out of the house on occasion like I do, where do you think and work best?

I have my CEO or vision time on Saturday evenings. This is when I have the house to myself for about two hours to reflect and think.

Your schedule will vary a lot from mine. It will depend on your most productive hours as well as the situations in which you think and work best.

Once you identify this, schedule project tasks here. Here's a snapshot of my schedule and how the 4 (+1) tasks integrate into a calendar.

8-9 AM: Marketing Bucket

9-10 AM: Non-Negotiable Bucket

2-4 PM: Project Bucket (This is my most productive time slot)

Sunday 5-6 PM: (+1) CEO Bucket

Identify what your major time blocks are by shading in the diagram. If yours varies day to day, draw the time circle into your daily calendar.

BUCKET	OPTIMAL TIME BLOCK

WEEKDAYS

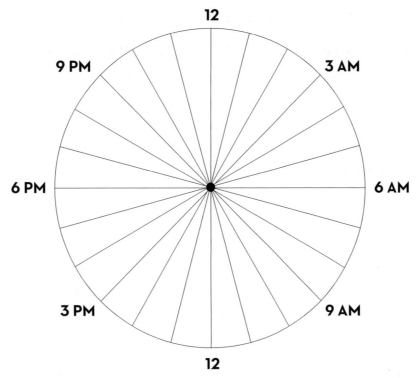

WEEKENDS

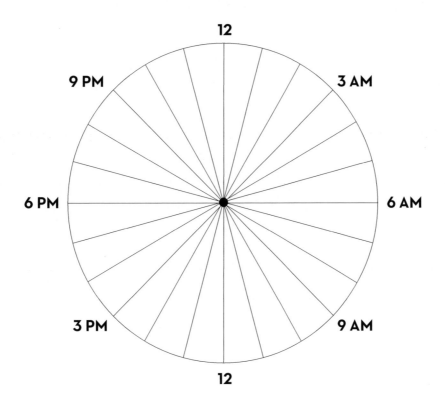

With this foundation in place, it's now
time to start planning and creating
compelling content!

SHARE YOUR PROGRESS

You're equipped with everything you need
to make the best use of this planner, and I
can't wait to see what you create. Tag me
@meerakothand with a picture of this planner
as you're working through it.

Meera

MEERAKOTHAND.COM

@MEERAKOTHAND

/MEERAKOTHAND

/MEERAKOTHAND

MEERA@MEERAKOTHAND.COM

YOUR YEAR AT A GLANCE

What new products do you want to create this year?

What new services do you want to offer this year?

What will you do to grow your community and audience this year? Planning to run new challenges or events?

Who do you want to work with or collaborate with this year? This list could also have names of influencers you want to connect and build a relationship with.

NAME OF PERSON / BRAND	SITE / URL	POTENTIAL PROJECT / IDEA

What's on your course/self-development/product wish list?

Before you answer this, consider the following questions:

- Will it move your blog + business forward?

  If you're not tech or design savvy and it's an element that's holding your business back, you may want to invest in tools that make design and tech easier for you.

- Will it save you time?

  If you're a fashion or food blogger and you rely on Instagram heavily as a platform to connect with your audience, you may want to invest in a scheduling tool to save you time.

- Is there a deal or special discount?

- Is there a recurring fee?

  Recurring fees are charged every month. If there is a similar product with a flat fee, do a comparison to see which is better.

- Is it relevant for the stage you are in?

  Will you have time to implement and put into practice what you learn in the course? Is this something you need for the stage you are in? If the answer is no, consider whether you really need this course at this point in time.

NAME OF COURSE/PRODUCT	TENTATIVE LAUNCH/ BUY DATE	COST

WHERE DO YOU WANT YOUR BRAND TO BE FEATURED? LIST PUBLICATIONS, WEBSITES, AND PODCASTS YOU WANT TO TARGET.

What's your revenue goal for the year?

Revenue is the sum total of what your business/
blog generates in earnings. Income is your personal
paycheck. It's the money in the business you send
back to yourself in exchange for the work you do.
If you are paying yourself a monthly income, add it
to the table on the next page. Dig into any existing
numbers to work through this table.

MONTHLY INCOME			
ANNUAL INCOME			

NAME OF OFFER	COPIES SOLD/ STUDENTS SIGNED UP	MONTHLY REVENUE	ANNUAL REVENUE

	SOURCE	MONTHLY REVENUE	ANNUAL REVENUE
AFFILIATE MARKETING			
SPONSORED POSTS			
TOTAL			

Will you be able to meet your annual revenue goals?

What can you do to make up for the shortfall if any?

DRAW IN YOUR OWN
REVENUE TABLES

REVENUE

ESTIMATED BUSINESS EXPENSES FOR THE YEAR (HOSTING, EMAIL SERVICE PROVIDER, ETC.)	
EXPENSE	AMOUNT

What goals or objectives, when achieved, will make your blog and business look like an absolute success this year?

1

2

3

4

5

6

Plug in your big projects, promotions, and tentative launches into the relevant months.

JANUARY	FEBRUARY	MARCH

APRIL	MAY	JUNE

JULY	AUGUST	SEPTEMBER

OCTOBER	NOVEMBER	DECEMBER

Based on these key projects and dates, what themes/campaigns and end goals will you have?

MONTH

CAMPAIGN / THEME

END GOAL

MONTH

CAMPAIGN / THEME

END GOAL

MONTH

CAMPAIGN / THEME

END GOAL

MONTH

CAMPAIGN / THEME

END GOAL

MONTH

CAMPAIGN / THEME

END GOAL

MONTH

CAMPAIGN / THEME

END GOAL

MONTH

CAMPAIGN / THEME

END GOAL

MONTH

CAMPAIGN / THEME

END GOAL

MONTH

CAMPAIGN / THEME

END GOAL

MONTH

CAMPAIGN / THEME

END GOAL

MONTH

CAMPAIGN / THEME

END GOAL

MONTH

CAMPAIGN / THEME

END GOAL

NO MATTER HOW MANY MISTAKES YOU MAKE OR HOW SLOW YOU PROGRESS, YOU ARE STILL WAY AHEAD OF EVERYONE WHO ISN'T TRYING.

TONY ROBBINS

PLAN YOUR QUARTER

01

What business stage are you in?

STARTUP STAGE 1	STARTUP STAGE 2	GROWTH STAGE 1	GROWTH STAGE 2	SCALE STAGE 1	SCALE STAGE 2
✓	◯	◯	◯	◯	◯

List 3 goals you want to achieve by the end of this quarter. Does every goal help you reach your stage milestone? If it doesn't, rethink your goal.

Nov
Dec
Jan
Feb
Mar

GOAL 1 Increase Email 500 1500

LIST EVERY TASK YOU CAN THINK OF TO COMPLETE YOUR GOAL

- optin / Lead Magnet -
- Mastermind
  nurturing sequence
  Content ups
  Pinterest
-

GOAL 2 Make 1st $1,000 $15,000

LIST EVERY TASK YOU CAN THINK OF TO COMPLETE YOUR GOAL

SM Cal
Content Runway
Affiliate Work

GOAL 3 Increase Web traffic

LIST EVERY TASK YOU CAN THINK OF TO COMPLETE YOUR GOAL

Pinterest -
Masterminds - Content
Mastermind List Building
Instagram
FB Group Collaboration

List any key projects and their deadlines for this quarter.

PROJECT/CAMPAIGN	DEADLINE	SPRINT (Y /N)	TENTATIVE SPRINT DATE
Social Media Calendar	11/10	y	
Content Runway	12/31	y	
Pinterest	ongoing		
Instagram .	ongoing	launch 8/1	

LIST ANY LOW-HANGING FRUIT IDEAS YOU HAVE FOR THIS QUARTER	
Affiliate Wah	- Build over Holiday
Guest Pod casts/ FB collab	Jan -

What's your campaign or theme for the month?

theme
Dec - Social media
Cmkat planning 2022

List 3 things you hope to achieve by the end of the month:

GOAL 1	Grow Email list 500

LIST EVERY TASK YOU CAN THINK OF TO COMPLETE YOUR GOAL

- Mastermind
- Lead Magnet
- Blog posts
- Pinterest

GOAL 2	Make 1st 6,000

LIST EVERY TASK YOU CAN THINK OF TO COMPLETE YOUR GOAL

- Social Media Calendar
- Content Runway - Launch | 1/15/2022

GOAL 3	Increase Web traffic 500 visitors

LIST EVERY TASK YOU CAN THINK OF TO COMPLETE YOUR GOAL

- Pinterest -
- Instagram -

CAMPAIGN ONE-SHEET

GOAL OF THE CAMPAIGN	Pre launch Artical Social Media Calendar

WHAT CONTENT WILL SUPPORT THIS CAMPAIGN AND HELP IT REACH ITS GOALS?

Prompts:
What questions are they researching at this stage?
What do they need to know before buying product/service?
What do they need to believe before buying product/service?
What are they confused about?
Answer popular question ___.
Do they need to understand ___?
Do they need to see __ as a viable solution?
Do they need to believe___?

What marketing assets do you need for this campaign? List down everything you can think of. Put a check mark against assets you can reuse.

BLOG POSTS		VIDEOS		LANDING PAGES		EMAILS		SOCIAL MEDIA IMAGES		OTHERS	
4 Posts	☑	FB Lives SMC	○	Challenge Landing Page SMC	☑	Confirmation Email	☑		☑	Facebook Ads	○
	☑		○	Landing Page SM 7nbo	○	Delivery	○		☑	SMcal	☑
	○		○	upsell SMC	○	welcome	○		☑	sm antr w/ upsell	☑
	○		○		○	nurturi	○		☑	Master Class.	○
	○		○		○		○		☑		○
	○		○		○		○		☑		○

WHAT DO YOU NEED TO DO TO ATTRACT PEOPLE TO THIS CAMPAIGN?

Create a landing page and promote on Pinterest.
Create 4-6 pin images.
Share 1 carousel post on IG.

Pinterest - need campaign spt

LIST ALL MAINTENANCE TASKS FOR THE MONTH

LIST ALL MARKETING TASKS FOR THE MONTH

E.g. Pitch Podcast X

Pinterest:
Launch Instagram 10/1
FB Lives 1 inst
Ad -
emails

LIST ALL PROJECT TASKS FOR THE MONTH

Blog posts
Email

LIST IMPORTANT DATES FOR THE MONTH

List all launch dates, affiliate promotions, collaborations, sales, etc.

What content will support your goals and/or campaign for this month? Use your campaign one-sheet for guidance. Include any audios, videos and images that you may be repurposing your content into the table as well.

DEADLINE	TITLE
16/03/XX	*Why you need a content plan: 5 Steps to create your brilliant content plan*

FORMAT	GOAL OF CONTENT / CALL TO ACTION	CONTENT UPGRADE	OUTLINE	DRAFT	EDIT	PUBLISH	REPURPOSE
Blog Post	Awareness - why a content plan is important	Checklist	○	○	✓	○	○
			○	○	○	○	○
			○	○	○	○	○
			○	○	○	○	○
			○	○	○	○	○
			○	○	○	○	○
			○	○	○	○	○
			○	○	○	○	○
			○	○	○	○	○
			○	○	○	○	○
			○	○	○	○	○
			○	○	○	○	○
			○	○	○	○	○
			○	○	○	○	○
			○	○	○	○	○
			○	○	○	○	○
			○	○	○	○	○
			○	○	○	○	○
			○	○	○	○	○
			○	○	○	○	○

What email content will support your goals and/or campaign for this month? Use your Campaign One-Sheet for guidance. Brainstorm at least 3 subject lines for each email.

GIST OF EMAIL CONTENT	SUBJECT LINE(S)

GOAL/CALL TO ACTION IN EMAIL	SEND DATE	OUTLINE	DRAFT	EDIT	SCHEDULE
Get on the wait list (build awareness for upcoming offer)		◯	◯	◯	◯
		◯	◯	◯	◯
		◯	◯	◯	◯
		◯	◯	◯	◯
		◯	◯	◯	◯
		◯	◯	◯	◯
		◯	◯	◯	◯
		◯	◯	◯	◯
		◯	◯	◯	◯
		◯	◯	◯	◯
		◯	◯	◯	◯

YOUR CREATE SPACE

YOUR CREATE SPACE

MONTH AT A GLANCE

Plug your tasks, key dates and projects for the month into the overview. Are you doing a sprint? Block it off in the calendar.

MONDAY	TUESDAY	WEDNESDAY	THURSDAY

FRIDAY	SATURDAY	SUNDAY

REMINDERS / NOTES

YOUR CEO / VISION SPACE

REVIEW YOUR MONTH

	THIS MONTH	LAST MONTH	+/- CHANGE
EMAIL SUBSCRIBERS			
PAGEVIEWS			
BOUNCE RATE			
5 MOST POPULAR POSTS (IN GOOGLE ANALYTICS)			
AVERAGE SESSION TIME			
TOP 5 TRAFFIC REFERRERS			

Track each of your emails sent out this month.

SUBJECT LINE	OPEN RATE	CLICK RATE

EXPENSES	AMOUNT
TOTAL	

REVENUE SOURCE	AMOUNT
TOTAL	

	THIS MONTH	LAST MONTH	+/- CHANGE
Facebook			
Twitter			
Instagram			
LinkedIn			
Pinterest			
YouTube			

CAMPAIGN ANALYSIS

What do you need to take note of the next time you run this same campaign?

What ideas do you have for future content pieces? (Explore the questions that your audience raised during the campaign.)

What can you do to achieve better results?

How much revenue did your campaign earn (if applicable)?

Did you meet your sales target (if applicable)?   YES   NO

How did it compare to previous campaigns you ran (if applicable)?

If you didn't meet your revenue target, try to pinpoint why this was so (if applicable). For example, maybe you didn't have enough people going through your campaign to meet the goal? Or your sales page didn't convert, although you had a healthy click-through rate?

The following will give you clues:

• High impressions, but low conversions

• High open rate, but low click-through rate

LET'S PLAN MONTH

What's your campaign or theme for the month?

List 3 things you hope to achieve by the end of the month:

GOAL 1

LIST EVERY TASK YOU CAN THINK OF TO COMPLETE YOUR GOAL

GOAL 2

LIST EVERY TASK YOU CAN THINK OF TO COMPLETE YOUR GOAL

GOAL 3

LIST EVERY TASK YOU CAN THINK OF TO COMPLETE YOUR GOAL

CAMPAIGN ONE-SHEET

GOAL OF THE CAMPAIGN	

WHAT CONTENT WILL SUPPORT THIS CAMPAIGN AND HELP IT REACH ITS GOALS?

What marketing assets do you need for this campaign? List down everything you can think of. Put a check mark against assets you can reuse.

BLOG POSTS	VIDEOS	LANDING PAGES	EMAILS	SOCIAL MEDIA IMAGES	OTHERS
○	○	○	○	○	○
○	○	○	○	○	○
○	○	○	○	○	○
○	○	○	○	○	○
○	○	○	○	○	○
○	○	○	○	○	○

WHAT DO YOU NEED TO DO TO ATTRACT PEOPLE TO THIS CAMPAIGN?

LIST ALL MAINTENANCE TASKS FOR THE MONTH

LIST ALL MARKETING TASKS FOR THE MONTH

LIST ALL PROJECT TASKS FOR THE MONTH

LIST IMPORTANT DATES FOR THE MONTH

What content will support your goals and/or campaign for this month? Use your campaign one-sheet for guidance. Include any audios, videos and images that you may be repurposing your content into the table as well.

DEADLINE	TITLE

FORMAT	GOAL OF CONTENT / CALL TO ACTION	CONTENT UPGRADE	OUTLINE	DRAFT	EDIT	PUBLISH	REPURPOSE
			○	○	○	○	○
			○	○	○	○	○
			○	○	○	○	○
			○	○	○	○	○
			○	○	○	○	○
			○	○	○	○	○
			○	○	○	○	○
			○	○	○	○	○
			○	○	○	○	○
			○	○	○	○	○
			○	○	○	○	○
			○	○	○	○	○
			○	○	○	○	○
			○	○	○	○	○
			○	○	○	○	○
			○	○	○	○	○
			○	○	○	○	○
			○	○	○	○	○
			○	○	○	○	○

What email content will support your goals and/or campaign for this month? Use your Campaign One-Sheet for guidance. Brainstorm at least 3 subject lines for each email.

GIST OF EMAIL CONTENT	SUBJECT LINE(S)

GOAL/CALL TO ACTION IN EMAIL	SEND DATE	OUTLINE	DRAFT	EDIT	SCHEDULE
		○	○	○	○
		○	○	○	○
		○	○	○	○
		○	○	○	○
		○	○	○	○
		○	○	○	○
		○	○	○	○
		○	○	○	○
		○	○	○	○
		○	○	○	○
		○	○	○	○

YOUR CREATE SPACE

MONTH AT A GLANCE

Plug your tasks, key dates and projects for the month into the overview. Are you doing a sprint? Block it off in the calendar.

MONDAY	TUESDAY	WEDNESDAY	THURSDAY

FRIDAY	SATURDAY	SUNDAY

REMINDERS / NOTES

YOUR CEO / VISION SPACE

REVIEW YOUR MONTH

	THIS MONTH	LAST MONTH	+/- CHANGE
EMAIL SUBSCRIBERS			
PAGEVIEWS			
BOUNCE RATE			
5 MOST POPULAR POSTS (IN GOOGLE ANALYTICS)			
AVERAGE SESSION TIME			
TOP 5 TRAFFIC REFERRERS			

Track each of your emails sent out this month.

SUBJECT LINE	OPEN RATE	CLICK RATE

EXPENSES	AMOUNT
TOTAL	

REVENUE SOURCE	AMOUNT
TOTAL	

	THIS MONTH	LAST MONTH	+/- CHANGE
Facebook			
Twitter			
Instagram			
LinkedIn			
Pinterest			
YouTube			

CAMPAIGN ANALYSIS

What do you need to take note of the next time you run this same campaign?

What ideas do you have for future content pieces? (Explore the questions that your audience raised during the campaign.)

What can you do to achieve better results?

How much revenue did your campaign earn (if applicable)?

Did you meet your sales target (if applicable)? YES NO

How did it compare to previous campaigns you ran (if applicable)?

If you didn't meet your revenue target, try to pinpoint why this was so (if applicable). For example, maybe you didn't have enough people going through your campaign to meet the goal? Or your sales page didn't convert, although you had a healthy click-through rate?

The following will give you clues:

• High impressions, but low conversions

• High open rate, but low click-through rate

LET'S PLAN MONTH

What's your campaign or theme for the month?

List 3 things you hope to achieve by the end of the month:

GOAL 1

LIST EVERY TASK YOU CAN THINK OF TO COMPLETE YOUR GOAL

GOAL 2

LIST EVERY TASK YOU CAN THINK OF TO COMPLETE YOUR GOAL

GOAL 3

LIST EVERY TASK YOU CAN THINK OF TO COMPLETE YOUR GOAL

CAMPAIGN ONE-SHEET

GOAL OF THE CAMPAIGN

WHAT CONTENT WILL SUPPORT THIS CAMPAIGN AND HELP IT REACH ITS GOALS?

What marketing assets do you need for this campaign? List down everything you can think of. Put a check mark against assets you can reuse.

BLOG POSTS	VIDEOS	LANDING PAGES	EMAILS	SOCIAL MEDIA IMAGES	OTHERS
○	○	○	○	○	○
○	○	○	○	○	○
○	○	○	○	○	○
○	○	○	○	○	○
○	○	○	○	○	○
○	○	○	○	○	○

WHAT DO YOU NEED TO DO TO ATTRACT PEOPLE TO THIS CAMPAIGN?

LIST ALL MAINTENANCE TASKS FOR THE MONTH

LIST ALL MARKETING TASKS FOR THE MONTH

LIST ALL PROJECT TASKS FOR THE MONTH

LIST IMPORTANT DATES FOR THE MONTH

What content will support your goals and/or campaign for this month? Use your campaign one-sheet for guidance. Include any audios, videos and images that you may be repurposing your content into the table as well.

DEADLINE	TITLE

What content will support your goals and/or campaign for this month? Use your campaign one-sheet for guidance. Include any audios, videos and images that you may be repurposing your content into the table as well.

FORMAT	GOAL OF CONTENT / CALL TO ACTION	CONTENT UPGRADE	OUTLINE	DRAFT	EDIT	PUBLISH	REPURPOSE
			○	○	○	○	○
			○	○	○	○	○
			○	○	○	○	○
			○	○	○	○	○
			○	○	○	○	○
			○	○	○	○	○
			○	○	○	○	○
			○	○	○	○	○
			○	○	○	○	○
			○	○	○	○	○
			○	○	○	○	○
			○	○	○	○	○
			○	○	○	○	○
			○	○	○	○	○
			○	○	○	○	○
			○	○	○	○	○
			○	○	○	○	○
			○	○	○	○	○
			○	○	○	○	○

What email content will support your goals and/or campaign for this month? Use your Campaign One-Sheet for guidance. Brainstorm at least 3 subject lines for each email.

GIST OF EMAIL CONTENT	SUBJECT LINE(S)

What email content will support your goals and/or campaign for this month? Use your Campaign One-Sheet for guidance. Brainstorm at least 3 subject lines for each email.

GOAL/CALL TO ACTION IN EMAIL	SEND DATE	OUTLINE	DRAFT	EDIT	SCHEDULE
		○	○	○	○
		○	○	○	○
		○	○	○	○
		○	○	○	○
		○	○	○	○
		○	○	○	○
		○	○	○	○
		○	○	○	○
		○	○	○	○
		○	○	○	○
		○	○	○	○

YOUR CREATE SPACE

YOUR CREATE SPACE

MONTH AT A GLANCE

Plug your tasks, key dates and projects for the month into the overview. Are you doing a sprint? Block it off in the calendar.

MONDAY	TUESDAY	WEDNESDAY	THURSDAY

FRIDAY	SATURDAY	SUNDAY

REMINDERS / NOTES

YOUR CEO / VISION SPACE

REVIEW YOUR MONTH

	THIS MONTH	LAST MONTH	+/- CHANGE
EMAIL SUBSCRIBERS			
PAGEVIEWS			
BOUNCE RATE			
5 MOST POPULAR POSTS (IN GOOGLE ANALYTICS)			
AVERAGE SESSION TIME			
TOP 5 TRAFFIC REFERRERS			

Track each of your emails sent out this month.

SUBJECT LINE	OPEN RATE	CLICK RATE

EXPENSES	AMOUNT
TOTAL	

REVENUE SOURCE	AMOUNT
TOTAL	

	THIS MONTH	LAST MONTH	+/- CHANGE
Facebook			
Twitter			
Instagram			
LinkedIn			
Pinterest			
YouTube			

CAMPAIGN ANALYSIS

What do you need to take note of the next time you run this same campaign?

What ideas do you have for future content pieces? (Explore the questions that your audience raised during the campaign.)

What can you do to achieve better results?

How much revenue did your campaign earn (if applicable)?

Did you meet your sales target (if applicable)?   YES   NO

How did it compare to previous campaigns you ran (if applicable)?

If you didn't meet your revenue target, try to pinpoint why this was so (if applicable). For example, maybe you didn't have enough people going through your campaign to meet the goal? Or your sales page didn't convert, although you had a healthy click-through rate?

The following will give you clues:

• High impressions, but low conversions

• High open rate, but low click-through rate

REVIEW
YOUR QUARTER

01

What worked well for you this quarter? (E.g., content that received a lot of comments? A spike in email subscribers?)

How can you replicate these results?

What obstacles are you facing in achieving your goals? Why is it difficult?

Did this quarter help you get closer to your annual objectives?

What can you try to overcome them?

Track the content you published this quarter. How well did it do on your most important social media platform? Track the number of opt-ins each content upgrade received.

CONTENT	SOCIAL SHARES	SIGN-UPS / OPT-INS	COMMENTS

LIST YOUR TOP 5 SUBJECT LINES FOR THIS QUARTER			
SUBJECT LINE	OPEN RATE	CLICK RATE	SUBSCRIBER ENGAGEMENT

LIST YOUR TOP 5 MOST POPULAR CONTENT UPGRADES FOR THIS QUARTER	SUBSCRIBERS

LET'S REVIEW YOUR CONTENT STRATEGY FOR THE QUARTER

Do you see any patterns in the type of content that attract an audience to your site? What can you learn about the type of content people want to read from you?

How can you capitalize on the success of these content pieces? (Examples: Add content upgrades, develop a related product, create similar content, repurpose existing content.)

LET'S REVIEW YOUR EMAIL STRATEGY FOR THE QUARTER

Do you see any patterns in the type of subject lines that worked well for your list? (Examples: Showing a result, using odd and specific numbers, highlighting benefits, expressing curiosity, showing your personal side, raising a question.)

Which emails received the most engagement and replies from your list? Can you tell why?

What opt-in incentive/landing page is working in terms of conversion rate? Keep it status quo or change it up?

Do you need to clean your list? (Re-engage or delete subscribers who haven't opened or clicked on your emails in 3 months or more.)

Do you need to make changes to how your website is optimized? (E.g., Are there any posts with lots of traffic but not converting to subscribers? Do you need to add extra opt-in forms? Do you need to add testimonials to a landing page?)

Are there any emails with a high unsubscribe rate? Can you tell why?

Do you see any patterns in the type of content upgrades that get the most opt-ins?

Where did most subscribers come from?

PLAN YOUR QUARTER

02

What business stage are you in?

STARTUP STAGE 1	STARTUP STAGE 2	GROWTH STAGE 1	GROWTH STAGE 2	SCALE STAGE 1	SCALE STAGE 2
◯	◯	◯	◯	◯	◯

List 3 goals you want to achieve by the end of this quarter. Does every goal help you reach your stage milestone? If it doesn't, rethink your goal.

GOAL 1

LIST EVERY TASK YOU CAN THINK OF TO COMPLETE YOUR GOAL

GOAL 2

LIST EVERY TASK YOU CAN THINK OF TO COMPLETE YOUR GOAL

GOAL 3

LIST EVERY TASK YOU CAN THINK OF TO COMPLETE YOUR GOAL

List any key projects and their deadlines for this quarter.

PROJECT/CAMPAIGN	DEADLINE	SPRINT (Y /N)	TENTATIVE SPRINT DATE

LIST ANY LOW-HANGING FRUIT IDEAS YOU HAVE FOR THIS QUARTER

LET'S PLAN MONTH

What's your campaign or theme for the month?

List 3 things you hope to achieve by the end of the month:

GOAL 1

LIST EVERY TASK YOU CAN THINK OF TO COMPLETE YOUR GOAL

GOAL 2

LIST EVERY TASK YOU CAN THINK OF TO COMPLETE YOUR GOAL

GOAL 3

LIST EVERY TASK YOU CAN THINK OF TO COMPLETE YOUR GOAL

CAMPAIGN ONE-SHEET

GOAL OF THE CAMPAIGN	

WHAT CONTENT WILL SUPPORT THIS CAMPAIGN AND HELP IT REACH ITS GOALS?

What marketing assets do you need for this campaign? List down everything you can think of. Put a check mark against assets you can reuse.

BLOG POSTS	VIDEOS	LANDING PAGES	EMAILS	SOCIAL MEDIA IMAGES	OTHERS
○	○	○	○	○	○
○	○	○	○	○	○
○	○	○	○	○	○
○	○	○	○	○	○
○	○	○	○	○	○
○	○	○	○	○	○

WHAT DO YOU NEED TO DO TO ATTRACT PEOPLE TO THIS CAMPAIGN?

LIST ALL MAINTENANCE TASKS FOR THE MONTH

LIST ALL MARKETING TASKS FOR THE MONTH

LIST ALL PROJECT TASKS FOR THE MONTH

LIST IMPORTANT DATES FOR THE MONTH

What content will support your goals and/or campaign for this month? Use your campaign one-sheet for guidance. Include any audios, videos and images that you may be repurposing your content into the table as well.

DEADLINE	TITLE

FORMAT	GOAL OF CONTENT / CALL TO ACTION	CONTENT UPGRADE	OUTLINE	DRAFT	EDIT	PUBLISH	REPURPOSE
			○	○	○	○	○
			○	○	○	○	○
			○	○	○	○	○
			○	○	○	○	○
			○	○	○	○	○
			○	○	○	○	○
			○	○	○	○	○
			○	○	○	○	○
			○	○	○	○	○
			○	○	○	○	○
			○	○	○	○	○
			○	○	○	○	○
			○	○	○	○	○
			○	○	○	○	○
			○	○	○	○	○
			○	○	○	○	○
			○	○	○	○	○
			○	○	○	○	○
			○	○	○	○	○

What email content will support your goals and/or campaign for this month? Use your Campaign One-Sheet for guidance. Brainstorm at least 3 subject lines for each email.

GIST OF EMAIL CONTENT	SUBJECT LINE(S)

GOAL/CALL TO ACTION IN EMAIL	SEND DATE	OUTLINE	DRAFT	EDIT	SCHEDULE
		◯	◯	◯	◯
		◯	◯	◯	◯
		◯	◯	◯	◯
		◯	◯	◯	◯
		◯	◯	◯	◯
		◯	◯	◯	◯
		◯	◯	◯	◯
		◯	◯	◯	◯
		◯	◯	◯	◯
		◯	◯	◯	◯
		◯	◯	◯	◯

YOUR CREATE SPACE

YOUR CREATE SPACE

MONTH AT A GLANCE

Plug your tasks, key dates and projects for the month into the overview. Are you doing a sprint? Block it off in the calendar.

MONDAY	TUESDAY	WEDNESDAY	THURSDAY

FRIDAY	SATURDAY	SUNDAY

REMINDERS / NOTES

YOUR CEO / VISION SPACE

REVIEW YOUR MONTH

	THIS MONTH	LAST MONTH	+/- CHANGE
EMAIL SUBSCRIBERS			
PAGEVIEWS			
BOUNCE RATE			
5 MOST POPULAR POSTS (IN GOOGLE ANALYTICS)			
AVERAGE SESSION TIME			
TOP 5 TRAFFIC REFERRERS			

Track each of your emails sent out this month.

SUBJECT LINE	OPEN RATE	CLICK RATE

EXPENSES	AMOUNT
TOTAL	

REVENUE SOURCE	AMOUNT
TOTAL	

	THIS MONTH	LAST MONTH	+/- CHANGE
Facebook			
Twitter			
Instagram			
LinkedIn			
Pinterest			
YouTube			

CAMPAIGN ANALYSIS

What do you need to take note of the next time you run this same campaign?

What ideas do you have for future content pieces? (Explore the questions that your audience raised during the campaign.)

What can you do to achieve better results?

How much revenue did your campaign earn (if applicable)?

Did you meet your sales target (if applicable)?   YES   NO

How did it compare to previous campaigns you ran (if applicable)?

If you didn't meet your revenue target, try to pinpoint why this was so (if applicable). For example, maybe you didn't have enough people going through your campaign to meet the goal? Or your sales page didn't convert, although you had a healthy click-through rate?

The following will give you clues:

• High impressions, but low conversions
• High open rate, but low click-through rate

LET'S PLAN MONTH

What's your campaign or theme for the month?

List 3 things you hope to achieve by the end of the month:

GOAL 1

LIST EVERY TASK YOU CAN THINK OF TO COMPLETE YOUR GOAL

GOAL 2

LIST EVERY TASK YOU CAN THINK OF TO COMPLETE YOUR GOAL

GOAL 3

LIST EVERY TASK YOU CAN THINK OF TO COMPLETE YOUR GOAL

CAMPAIGN ONE-SHEET

GOAL OF THE CAMPAIGN

WHAT CONTENT WILL SUPPORT THIS CAMPAIGN AND HELP IT REACH ITS GOALS?

What marketing assets do you need for this campaign? List down everything you can think of. Put a check mark against assets you can reuse.

BLOG POSTS	VIDEOS	LANDING PAGES	EMAILS	SOCIAL MEDIA IMAGES	OTHERS
○	○	○	○	○	○
○	○	○	○	○	○
○	○	○	○	○	○
○	○	○	○	○	○
○	○	○	○	○	○
○	○	○	○	○	○

WHAT DO YOU NEED TO DO TO ATTRACT PEOPLE TO THIS CAMPAIGN?

LIST ALL MAINTENANCE TASKS FOR THE MONTH

LIST ALL MARKETING TASKS FOR THE MONTH

LIST ALL PROJECT TASKS FOR THE MONTH

LIST IMPORTANT DATES FOR THE MONTH

What content will support your goals and/or campaign for this month? Use your campaign one-sheet for guidance. Include any audios, videos and images that you may be repurposing your content into the table as well.

DEADLINE	TITLE

FORMAT	GOAL OF CONTENT / CALL TO ACTION	CONTENT UPGRADE	OUTLINE	DRAFT	EDIT	PUBLISH	REPURPOSE
			○	○	○	○	○
			○	○	○	○	○
			○	○	○	○	○
			○	○	○	○	○
			○	○	○	○	○
			○	○	○	○	○
			○	○	○	○	○
			○	○	○	○	○
			○	○	○	○	○
			○	○	○	○	○
			○	○	○	○	○
			○	○	○	○	○
			○	○	○	○	○
			○	○	○	○	○
			○	○	○	○	○
			○	○	○	○	○
			○	○	○	○	○
			○	○	○	○	○
			○	○	○	○	○

What email content will support your goals and/or campaign for this month? Use your Campaign One-Sheet for guidance. Brainstorm at least 3 subject lines for each email.

GIST OF EMAIL CONTENT	SUBJECT LINE(S)

GOAL/CALL TO ACTION IN EMAIL	SEND DATE	OUTLINE	DRAFT	EDIT	SCHEDULE
		○	○	○	○
		○	○	○	○
		○	○	○	○
		○	○	○	○
		○	○	○	○
		○	○	○	○
		○	○	○	○
		○	○	○	○
		○	○	○	○
		○	○	○	○
		○	○	○	○

YOUR CREATE SPACE

YOUR CREATE SPACE

MONTH AT A GLANCE

Plug your tasks, key dates and projects for the month into the overview. Are you doing a sprint? Block it off in the calendar.

MONDAY	TUESDAY	WEDNESDAY	THURSDAY

FRIDAY	SATURDAY	SUNDAY

REMINDERS / NOTES

YOUR CEO / VISION SPACE

REVIEW YOUR MONTH

	THIS MONTH	LAST MONTH	+/- CHANGE
EMAIL SUBSCRIBERS			
PAGEVIEWS			
BOUNCE RATE			
5 MOST POPULAR POSTS (IN GOOGLE ANALYTICS)			
AVERAGE SESSION TIME			
TOP 5 TRAFFIC REFERRERS			

Track each of your emails sent out this month.

SUBJECT LINE	OPEN RATE	CLICK RATE

EXPENSES	AMOUNT
TOTAL	

REVENUE SOURCE	AMOUNT
TOTAL	

	THIS MONTH	LAST MONTH	+/- CHANGE
Facebook			
Twitter			
Instagram			
LinkedIn			
Pinterest			
YouTube			

CAMPAIGN ANALYSIS

What do you need to take note of the next time you run this same campaign?

What ideas do you have for future content pieces? (Explore the questions that your audience raised during the campaign.)

What can you do to achieve better results?

How much revenue did your campaign earn (if applicable)?

Did you meet your sales target (if applicable)?   YES   NO

How did it compare to previous campaigns you ran (if applicable)?

If you didn't meet your revenue target, try to pinpoint why this was so (if applicable). For example, maybe you didn't have enough people going through your campaign to meet the goal? Or your sales page didn't convert, although you had a healthy click-through rate?

The following will give you clues:

• High impressions, but low conversions

• High open rate, but low click-through rate

What's your campaign or theme for the month?

List 3 things you hope to achieve by the end of the month:

GOAL 1

LIST EVERY TASK YOU CAN THINK OF TO COMPLETE YOUR GOAL

GOAL 2

LIST EVERY TASK YOU CAN THINK OF TO COMPLETE YOUR GOAL

GOAL 3

LIST EVERY TASK YOU CAN THINK OF TO COMPLETE YOUR GOAL

CAMPAIGN ONE-SHEET

GOAL OF THE CAMPAIGN	

WHAT CONTENT WILL SUPPORT THIS CAMPAIGN AND HELP IT REACH ITS GOALS?

What marketing assets do you need for this campaign? List down everything you can think of. Put a check mark against assets you can reuse.

BLOG POSTS	VIDEOS	LANDING PAGES	EMAILS	SOCIAL MEDIA IMAGES	OTHERS
○	○	○	○	○	○
○	○	○	○	○	○
○	○	○	○	○	○
○	○	○	○	○	○
○	○	○	○	○	○
○	○	○	○	○	○

WHAT DO YOU NEED TO DO TO ATTRACT PEOPLE TO THIS CAMPAIGN?

LIST ALL MAINTENANCE TASKS FOR THE MONTH

LIST ALL MARKETING TASKS FOR THE MONTH

LIST ALL PROJECT TASKS FOR THE MONTH

LIST IMPORTANT DATES FOR THE MONTH

What content will support your goals and/or campaign for this month? Use your campaign one-sheet for guidance. Include any audios, videos and images that you may be repurposing your content into the table as well.

DEADLINE	TITLE

FORMAT	GOAL OF CONTENT / CALL TO ACTION	CONTENT UPGRADE	OUTLINE	DRAFT	EDIT	PUBLISH	REPURPOSE
			○	○	○	○	○
			○	○	○	○	○
			○	○	○	○	○
			○	○	○	○	○
			○	○	○	○	○
			○	○	○	○	○
			○	○	○	○	○
			○	○	○	○	○
			○	○	○	○	○
			○	○	○	○	○
			○	○	○	○	○
			○	○	○	○	○
			○	○	○	○	○
			○	○	○	○	○
			○	○	○	○	○
			○	○	○	○	○
			○	○	○	○	○
			○	○	○	○	○
			○	○	○	○	○
			○	○	○	○	○

What email content will support your goals and/or campaign for this month? Use your Campaign One-Sheet for guidance. Brainstorm at least 3 subject lines for each email.

GIST OF EMAIL CONTENT	SUBJECT LINE(S)

GOAL/CALL TO ACTION IN EMAIL	SEND DATE	OUTLINE	DRAFT	EDIT	SCHEDULE
		○	○	○	○
		○	○	○	○
		○	○	○	○
		○	○	○	○
		○	○	○	○
		○	○	○	○
		○	○	○	○
		○	○	○	○
		○	○	○	○
		○	○	○	○
		○	○	○	○

YOUR CREATE SPACE

YOUR CREATE SPACE

MONTH AT A GLANCE

Plug your tasks, key dates and projects for the month into the overview. Are you doing a sprint? Block it off in the calendar.

MONDAY	TUESDAY	WEDNESDAY	THURSDAY

FRIDAY	SATURDAY	SUNDAY

YOUR CEO / VISION SPACE

REVIEW YOUR MONTH

	THIS MONTH	LAST MONTH	+/- CHANGE
EMAIL SUBSCRIBERS			
PAGEVIEWS			
BOUNCE RATE			
5 MOST POPULAR POSTS (IN GOOGLE ANALYTICS)			
AVERAGE SESSION TIME			
TOP 5 TRAFFIC REFERRERS			

Track each of your emails sent out this month.

SUBJECT LINE	OPEN RATE	CLICK RATE

EXPENSES	AMOUNT
TOTAL	

REVENUE SOURCE	AMOUNT
TOTAL	

	THIS MONTH	LAST MONTH	+/- CHANGE
Facebook			
Twitter			
Instagram			
LinkedIn			
Pinterest			
YouTube			

CAMPAIGN ANALYSIS

What do you need to take note of the next time you run this same campaign?

What ideas do you have for future content pieces? (Explore the questions that your audience raised during the campaign.)

What can you do to achieve better results?

How much revenue did your campaign earn (if applicable)?

Did you meet your sales target (if applicable)?   YES   NO

How did it compare to previous campaigns you ran (if applicable)?

If you didn't meet your revenue target, try to pinpoint why this was so (if applicable). For example, maybe you didn't have enough people going through your campaign to meet the goal? Or your sales page didn't convert, although you had a healthy click-through rate?

The following will give you clues:

• High impressions, but low conversions

• High open rate, but low click-through rate

REVIEW
YOUR QUARTER

02

What worked well for you this quarter? (E.g., content that received a lot of comments? A spike in email subscribers?)

How can you replicate these results?

What obstacles are you facing in achieving your goals? Why is it difficult?

Did this quarter help you get closer to your annual objectives?

What can you try to overcome them?

Track the content you published this quarter. How well did it do on your most important social media platform? Track the number of opt-ins each content upgrade received.

CONTENT	SOCIAL SHARES	SIGN-UPS / OPT-INS	COMMENTS

LIST YOUR TOP 5 SUBJECT LINES FOR THIS QUARTER			
SUBJECT LINE	OPEN RATE	CLICK RATE	SUBSCRIBER ENGAGEMENT

LIST YOUR TOP 5 MOST POPULAR CONTENT UPGRADES FOR THIS QUARTER	SUBSCRIBERS

LET'S REVIEW YOUR CONTENT STRATEGY FOR THE QUARTER

Do you see any patterns in the type of content that attract an audience to your site? What can you learn about the type of content people want to read from you?

How can you capitalize on the success of these content pieces? (Examples: Add content upgrades, develop a related product, create similar content, repurpose existing content.)

LET'S REVIEW YOUR EMAIL STRATEGY FOR THE QUARTER

Do you see any patterns in the type of subject lines that worked well for your list? (Examples: Showing a result, using odd and specific numbers, highlighting benefits, expressing curiosity, showing your personal side, raising a question.)

Which emails received the most engagement and replies from your list? Can you tell why?

What opt-in incentive/landing page is working in terms of conversion rate? Keep it status quo or change it up?

Do you need to clean your list? (Re-engage or delete subscribers who haven't opened or clicked on your emails in 3 months or more.)

Do you need to make changes to how your website is optimized? (E.g., Are there any posts with lots of traffic but not converting to subscribers? Do you need to add extra opt-in forms? Do you need to add testimonials to a landing page?)

Are there any emails with a high unsubscribe rate? Can you tell why?

Do you see any patterns in the type of content upgrades that get the most opt-ins?

Where did most subscribers come from?

PLAN YOUR QUARTER

03

What business stage are you in?

STARTUP STAGE 1	STARTUP STAGE 2	GROWTH STAGE 1	GROWTH STAGE 2	SCALE STAGE 1	SCALE STAGE 2
◯	◯	◯	◯	◯	◯

List 3 goals you want to achieve by the end of this quarter. Does every goal help you reach your stage milestone? If it doesn't, rethink your goal.

GOAL 1

LIST EVERY TASK YOU CAN THINK OF TO COMPLETE YOUR GOAL

GOAL 2

LIST EVERY TASK YOU CAN THINK OF TO COMPLETE YOUR GOAL

GOAL 3

LIST EVERY TASK YOU CAN THINK OF TO COMPLETE YOUR GOAL

List any key projects and their deadlines for this quarter.

PROJECT/CAMPAIGN	DEADLINE	SPRINT (Y /N)	TENTATIVE SPRINT DATE

LIST ANY LOW-HANGING FRUIT IDEAS YOU HAVE FOR THIS QUARTER

LET'S PLAN MONTH

What's your campaign or theme for the month?

List 3 things you hope to achieve by the end of the month:

GOAL 1

LIST EVERY TASK YOU CAN THINK OF TO COMPLETE YOUR GOAL

GOAL 2

LIST EVERY TASK YOU CAN THINK OF TO COMPLETE YOUR GOAL

GOAL 3

LIST EVERY TASK YOU CAN THINK OF TO COMPLETE YOUR GOAL

CAMPAIGN ONE-SHEET

GOAL OF THE CAMPAIGN	

WHAT CONTENT WILL SUPPORT THIS CAMPAIGN AND HELP IT REACH ITS GOALS?

What marketing assets do you need for this campaign? List down everything you can think of. Put a check mark against assets you can reuse.

BLOG POSTS	VIDEOS	LANDING PAGES	EMAILS	SOCIAL MEDIA IMAGES	OTHERS
○	○	○	○	○	○
○	○	○	○	○	○
○	○	○	○	○	○
○	○	○	○	○	○
○	○	○	○	○	○
○	○	○	○	○	○

WHAT DO YOU NEED TO DO TO ATTRACT PEOPLE TO THIS CAMPAIGN?

LIST ALL MAINTENANCE TASKS FOR THE MONTH

LIST ALL MARKETING TASKS FOR THE MONTH

LIST ALL PROJECT TASKS FOR THE MONTH

LIST IMPORTANT DATES FOR THE MONTH

What content will support your goals and/or campaign for this month? Use your campaign one-sheet for guidance. Include any audios, videos and images that you may be repurposing your content into the table as well.

DEADLINE	TITLE

FORMAT	GOAL OF CONTENT / CALL TO ACTION	CONTENT UPGRADE	OUTLINE	DRAFT	EDIT	PUBLISH	REPURPOSE
			○	○	○	○	○
			○	○	○	○	○
			○	○	○	○	○
			○	○	○	○	○
			○	○	○	○	○
			○	○	○	○	○
			○	○	○	○	○
			○	○	○	○	○
			○	○	○	○	○
			○	○	○	○	○
			○	○	○	○	○
			○	○	○	○	○
			○	○	○	○	○
			○	○	○	○	○
			○	○	○	○	○
			○	○	○	○	○
			○	○	○	○	○
			○	○	○	○	○
			○	○	○	○	○

What email content will support your goals and/or campaign for this month? Use your Campaign One-Sheet for guidance. Brainstorm at least 3 subject lines for each email.

GIST OF EMAIL CONTENT	SUBJECT LINE(S)

GOAL/CALL TO ACTION IN EMAIL	SEND DATE	OUTLINE	DRAFT	EDIT	SCHEDULE
		◯	◯	◯	◯
		◯	◯	◯	◯
		◯	◯	◯	◯
		◯	◯	◯	◯
		◯	◯	◯	◯
		◯	◯	◯	◯
		◯	◯	◯	◯
		◯	◯	◯	◯
		◯	◯	◯	◯
		◯	◯	◯	◯
		◯	◯	◯	◯

YOUR CREATE SPACE

YOUR CREATE SPACE

MONTH AT A GLANCE

Plug your tasks, key dates and projects for the month into the overview. Are you doing a sprint? Block it off in the calendar.

MONDAY	TUESDAY	WEDNESDAY	THURSDAY

FRIDAY	SATURDAY	SUNDAY

YOUR CEO / VISION SPACE

REVIEW YOUR MONTH

	THIS MONTH	LAST MONTH	+/- CHANGE
EMAIL SUBSCRIBERS			
PAGEVIEWS			
BOUNCE RATE			
5 MOST POPULAR POSTS (IN GOOGLE ANALYTICS)			
AVERAGE SESSION TIME			
TOP 5 TRAFFIC REFERRERS			

Track each of your emails sent out this month.

SUBJECT LINE	OPEN RATE	CLICK RATE

EXPENSES	AMOUNT
TOTAL	

REVENUE SOURCE	AMOUNT
TOTAL	

	THIS MONTH	LAST MONTH	+/- CHANGE
Facebook			
Twitter			
Instagram			
LinkedIn			
Pinterest			
YouTube			

CAMPAIGN ANALYSIS

What do you need to take note of the next time you run this same campaign?

What ideas do you have for future content pieces? (Explore the questions that your audience raised during the campaign.)

What can you do to achieve better results?

How much revenue did your campaign earn (if applicable)?

Did you meet your sales target (if applicable)?　　YES　　NO

How did it compare to previous campaigns you ran (if applicable)?

If you didn't meet your revenue target, try to pinpoint why this was so (if applicable). For example, maybe you didn't have enough people going through your campaign to meet the goal? Or your sales page didn't convert, although you had a healthy click-through rate?

The following will give you clues:

• High impressions, but low conversions

• High open rate, but low click-through rate

LET'S PLAN MONTH

What's your campaign or theme for the month?

List 3 things you hope to achieve by the end of the month:

GOAL 1

LIST EVERY TASK YOU CAN THINK OF TO COMPLETE YOUR GOAL

GOAL 2

LIST EVERY TASK YOU CAN THINK OF TO COMPLETE YOUR GOAL

GOAL 3

LIST EVERY TASK YOU CAN THINK OF TO COMPLETE YOUR GOAL

CAMPAIGN ONE-SHEET

GOAL OF THE CAMPAIGN	

WHAT CONTENT WILL SUPPORT THIS CAMPAIGN AND HELP IT REACH ITS GOALS?

What marketing assets do you need for this campaign? List down everything you can think of. Put a check mark against assets you can reuse.

BLOG POSTS	VIDEOS	LANDING PAGES	EMAILS	SOCIAL MEDIA IMAGES	OTHERS
○	○	○	○	○	○
○	○	○	○	○	○
○	○	○	○	○	○
○	○	○	○	○	○
○	○	○	○	○	○
○	○	○	○	○	○

WHAT DO YOU NEED TO DO TO ATTRACT PEOPLE TO THIS CAMPAIGN?

LIST ALL MAINTENANCE TASKS FOR THE MONTH

LIST ALL MARKETING TASKS FOR THE MONTH

LIST ALL PROJECT TASKS FOR THE MONTH

LIST IMPORTANT DATES FOR THE MONTH

What content will support your goals and/or campaign for this month? Use your campaign one-sheet for guidance. Include any audios, videos and images that you may be repurposing your content into the table as well.

DEADLINE	TITLE

FORMAT	GOAL OF CONTENT / CALL TO ACTION	CONTENT UPGRADE	OUTLINE	DRAFT	EDIT	PUBLISH	REPURPOSE
			○	○	○	○	○
			○	○	○	○	○
			○	○	○	○	○
			○	○	○	○	○
			○	○	○	○	○
			○	○	○	○	○
			○	○	○	○	○
			○	○	○	○	○
			○	○	○	○	○
			○	○	○	○	○
			○	○	○	○	○
			○	○	○	○	○
			○	○	○	○	○
			○	○	○	○	○
			○	○	○	○	○
			○	○	○	○	○
			○	○	○	○	○
			○	○	○	○	○
			○	○	○	○	○

What email content will support your goals and/or campaign for this month? Use your Campaign One-Sheet for guidance. Brainstorm at least 3 subject lines for each email.

GIST OF EMAIL CONTENT	SUBJECT LINE(S)

GOAL/CALL TO ACTION IN EMAIL	SEND DATE	OUTLINE	DRAFT	EDIT	SCHEDULE
		○	○	○	○
		○	○	○	○
		○	○	○	○
		○	○	○	○
		○	○	○	○
		○	○	○	○
		○	○	○	○
		○	○	○	○
		○	○	○	○
		○	○	○	○
		○	○	○	○

YOUR CREATE SPACE

YOUR CREATE SPACE

MONTH AT A GLANCE

Plug your tasks, key dates and projects for the month into the overview. Are you doing a sprint? Block it off in the calendar.

MONDAY	TUESDAY	WEDNESDAY	THURSDAY

FRIDAY	SATURDAY	SUNDAY

REMINDERS / NOTES

....
....
....
....
....
....
....
....
....
....
....
....
....
....
....
....
....
....
....

YOUR CEO / VISION SPACE

REVIEW YOUR MONTH

	THIS MONTH	LAST MONTH	+/- CHANGE
EMAIL SUBSCRIBERS			
PAGEVIEWS			
BOUNCE RATE			
5 MOST POPULAR POSTS (IN GOOGLE ANALYTICS)			
AVERAGE SESSION TIME			
TOP 5 TRAFFIC REFERRERS			

Track each of your emails sent out this month.

SUBJECT LINE	OPEN RATE	CLICK RATE

EXPENSES	AMOUNT
TOTAL	

REVENUE SOURCE	AMOUNT
TOTAL	

	THIS MONTH	LAST MONTH	+/- CHANGE
Facebook			
Twitter			
Instagram			
LinkedIn			
Pinterest			
YouTube			

CAMPAIGN ANALYSIS

What do you need to take note of the next time you run this same campaign?

What ideas do you have for future content pieces? (Explore the questions that your audience raised during the campaign.)

What can you do to achieve better results?

How much revenue did your campaign earn (if applicable)?

Did you meet your sales target (if applicable)?   YES   NO

How did it compare to previous campaigns you ran (if applicable)?

If you didn't meet your revenue target, try to pinpoint why this was so (if applicable). For example, maybe you didn't have enough people going through your campaign to meet the goal? Or your sales page didn't convert, although you had a healthy click-through rate?

The following will give you clues:

- High impressions, but low conversions
- High open rate, but low click-through rate

LET'S PLAN MONTH

What's your campaign or theme for the month?

List 3 things you hope to achieve by the end of the month:

GOAL 1

LIST EVERY TASK YOU CAN THINK OF TO COMPLETE YOUR GOAL

GOAL 2

LIST EVERY TASK YOU CAN THINK OF TO COMPLETE YOUR GOAL

GOAL 3

LIST EVERY TASK YOU CAN THINK OF TO COMPLETE YOUR GOAL

CAMPAIGN ONE-SHEET

GOAL OF THE CAMPAIGN	

WHAT CONTENT WILL SUPPORT THIS CAMPAIGN AND HELP IT REACH ITS GOALS?

What marketing assets do you need for this campaign? List down everything you can think of. Put a check mark against assets you can reuse.

BLOG POSTS	VIDEOS	LANDING PAGES	EMAILS	SOCIAL MEDIA IMAGES	OTHERS
○	○	○	○	○	○
○	○	○	○	○	○
○	○	○	○	○	○
○	○	○	○	○	○
○	○	○	○	○	○
○	○	○	○	○	○

WHAT DO YOU NEED TO DO TO ATTRACT PEOPLE TO THIS CAMPAIGN?

LIST ALL MAINTENANCE TASKS FOR THE MONTH

LIST ALL MARKETING TASKS FOR THE MONTH

LIST ALL PROJECT TASKS FOR THE MONTH

LIST IMPORTANT DATES FOR THE MONTH

What content will support your goals and/or campaign for this month? Use your campaign one-sheet for guidance. Include any audios, videos and images that you may be repurposing your content into the table as well.

DEADLINE	TITLE

FORMAT	GOAL OF CONTENT / CALL TO ACTION	CONTENT UPGRADE	OUTLINE	DRAFT	EDIT	PUBLISH	REPURPOSE
			○	○	○	○	○
			○	○	○	○	○
			○	○	○	○	○
			○	○	○	○	○
			○	○	○	○	○
			○	○	○	○	○
			○	○	○	○	○
			○	○	○	○	○
			○	○	○	○	○
			○	○	○	○	○
			○	○	○	○	○
			○	○	○	○	○
			○	○	○	○	○
			○	○	○	○	○
			○	○	○	○	○
			○	○	○	○	○
			○	○	○	○	○
			○	○	○	○	○
			○	○	○	○	○

What email content will support your goals and/or campaign for this month? Use your Campaign One-Sheet for guidance. Brainstorm at least 3 subject lines for each email.

GIST OF EMAIL CONTENT	SUBJECT LINE(S)

GOAL/CALL TO ACTION IN EMAIL	SEND DATE	OUTLINE	DRAFT	EDIT	SCHEDULE
		○	○	○	○
		○	○	○	○
		○	○	○	○
		○	○	○	○
		○	○	○	○
		○	○	○	○
		○	○	○	○
		○	○	○	○
		○	○	○	○
		○	○	○	○
		○	○	○	○

YOUR CREATE SPACE

YOUR CREATE SPACE

MONTH AT A GLANCE

Plug your tasks, key dates and projects for the month into the overview. Are you doing a sprint? Block it off in the calendar.

MONDAY	TUESDAY	WEDNESDAY	THURSDAY

FRIDAY	SATURDAY	SUNDAY

YOUR CEO / VISION SPACE

REVIEW YOUR MONTH

	THIS MONTH	LAST MONTH	+/- CHANGE
EMAIL SUBSCRIBERS			
PAGEVIEWS			
BOUNCE RATE			
5 MOST POPULAR POSTS (IN GOOGLE ANALYTICS)			
AVERAGE SESSION TIME			
TOP 5 TRAFFIC REFERRERS			

Track each of your emails sent out this month.

SUBJECT LINE	OPEN RATE	CLICK RATE

EXPENSES	AMOUNT
TOTAL	

REVENUE SOURCE	AMOUNT
TOTAL	

	THIS MONTH	LAST MONTH	+/- CHANGE
Facebook			
Twitter			
Instagram			
LinkedIn			
Pinterest			
YouTube			

CAMPAIGN ANALYSIS

What do you need to take note of the next time you run this same campaign?

What ideas do you have for future content pieces? (Explore the questions that your audience raised during the campaign.)

What can you do to achieve better results?

How much revenue did your campaign earn (if applicable)?

Did you meet your sales target (if applicable)?   YES   NO

How did it compare to previous campaigns you ran (if applicable)?

If you didn't meet your revenue target, try to pinpoint why this was so (if applicable). For example, maybe you didn't have enough people going through your campaign to meet the goal? Or your sales page didn't convert, although you had a healthy click-through rate?

The following will give you clues:

• High impressions, but low conversions
• High open rate, but low click-through rate

REVIEW
YOUR QUARTER

03

What worked well for you this quarter? (E.g., content that received a lot of comments? A spike in email subscribers?)

How can you replicate these results?

What obstacles are you facing in achieving your goals? Why is it difficult?

Did this quarter help you get closer to your annual objectives?

What can you try to overcome them?

Track the content you published this quarter. How well did it do on your most important social media platform? Track the number of opt-ins each content upgrade received.

CONTENT	SOCIAL SHARES	SIGN-UPS / OPT-INS	COMMENTS

LIST YOUR TOP 5 SUBJECT LINES FOR THIS QUARTER			
SUBJECT LINE	OPEN RATE	CLICK RATE	SUBSCRIBER ENGAGEMENT

LIST YOUR TOP 5 MOST POPULAR CONTENT UPGRADES FOR THIS QUARTER	SUBSCRIBERS

LET'S REVIEW YOUR CONTENT STRATEGY FOR THE QUARTER

Do you see any patterns in the type of content that attract an audience to your site? What can you learn about the type of content people want to read from you?

How can you capitalize on the success of these content pieces? (Examples: Add content upgrades, develop a related product, create similar content, repurpose existing content.)

LET'S REVIEW YOUR EMAIL STRATEGY FOR THE QUARTER

Do you see any patterns in the type of subject lines that worked well for your list? (Examples: Showing a result, using odd and specific numbers, highlighting benefits, expressing curiosity, showing your personal side, raising a question.)

Which emails received the most engagement and replies from your list? Can you tell why?

What opt-in incentive/landing page is working in terms of conversion rate? Keep it status quo or change it up?

Do you need to clean your list? (Re-engage or delete subscribers who haven't opened or clicked on your emails in 3 months or more.)

Do you need to make changes to how your website is optimized? (E.g., Are there any posts with lots of traffic but not converting to subscribers? Do you need to add extra opt-in forms? Do you need to add testimonials to a landing page?)

Are there any emails with a high unsubscribe rate? Can you tell why?

Do you see any patterns in the type of content upgrades that get the most opt-ins?

Where did most subscribers come from?

PLAN YOUR QUARTER

04

What business stage are you in?

STARTUP STAGE 1	STARTUP STAGE 2	GROWTH STAGE 1	GROWTH STAGE 2	SCALE STAGE 1	SCALE STAGE 2
◯	◯	◯	◯	◯	◯

List 3 goals you want to achieve by the end of this quarter. Does every goal help you reach your stage milestone? If it doesn't, rethink your goal.

GOAL 1

LIST EVERY TASK YOU CAN THINK OF TO COMPLETE YOUR GOAL

GOAL 2

LIST EVERY TASK YOU CAN THINK OF TO COMPLETE YOUR GOAL

GOAL 3

LIST EVERY TASK YOU CAN THINK OF TO COMPLETE YOUR GOAL

List any key projects and their deadlines for this quarter.

PROJECT/CAMPAIGN	DEADLINE	SPRINT (Y /N)	TENTATIVE SPRINT DATE

LIST ANY LOW-HANGING FRUIT IDEAS YOU HAVE FOR THIS QUARTER

LET'S PLAN MONTH

What's your campaign or theme for the month?

List 3 things you hope to achieve by the end of the month:

GOAL 1

LIST EVERY TASK YOU CAN THINK OF TO COMPLETE YOUR GOAL

GOAL 2

LIST EVERY TASK YOU CAN THINK OF TO COMPLETE YOUR GOAL

GOAL 3

LIST EVERY TASK YOU CAN THINK OF TO COMPLETE YOUR GOAL

CAMPAIGN ONE-SHEET

GOAL OF THE CAMPAIGN

WHAT CONTENT WILL SUPPORT THIS CAMPAIGN AND HELP IT REACH ITS GOALS?

What marketing assets do you need for this campaign? List down everything you can think of. Put a check mark against assets you can reuse.

BLOG POSTS	VIDEOS	LANDING PAGES	EMAILS	SOCIAL MEDIA IMAGES	OTHERS
○	○	○	○	○	○
○	○	○	○	○	○
○	○	○	○	○	○
○	○	○	○	○	○
○	○	○	○	○	○
○	○	○	○	○	○

WHAT DO YOU NEED TO DO TO ATTRACT PEOPLE TO THIS CAMPAIGN?

LIST ALL MAINTENANCE TASKS FOR THE MONTH

LIST ALL MARKETING TASKS FOR THE MONTH

LIST ALL PROJECT TASKS FOR THE MONTH

LIST IMPORTANT DATES FOR THE MONTH

What content will support your goals and/or campaign for this month? Use your campaign one-sheet for guidance. Include any audios, videos and images that you may be repurposing your content into the table as well.

DEADLINE	TITLE

FORMAT	GOAL OF CONTENT / CALL TO ACTION	CONTENT UPGRADE	OUTLINE	DRAFT	EDIT	PUBLISH	REPURPOSE
			○	○	○	○	○
			○	○	○	○	○
			○	○	○	○	○
			○	○	○	○	○
			○	○	○	○	○
			○	○	○	○	○
			○	○	○	○	○
			○	○	○	○	○
			○	○	○	○	○
			○	○	○	○	○
			○	○	○	○	○
			○	○	○	○	○
			○	○	○	○	○
			○	○	○	○	○
			○	○	○	○	○
			○	○	○	○	○
			○	○	○	○	○
			○	○	○	○	○
			○	○	○	○	○
			○	○	○	○	○

What email content will support your goals and/or campaign for this month? Use your Campaign One-Sheet for guidance. Brainstorm at least 3 subject lines for each email.

GIST OF EMAIL CONTENT	SUBJECT LINE(S)

GOAL/CALL TO ACTION IN EMAIL	SEND DATE	OUTLINE	DRAFT	EDIT	SCHEDULE
		◯	◯	◯	◯
		◯	◯	◯	◯
		◯	◯	◯	◯
		◯	◯	◯	◯
		◯	◯	◯	◯
		◯	◯	◯	◯
		◯	◯	◯	◯
		◯	◯	◯	◯
		◯	◯	◯	◯
		◯	◯	◯	◯

YOUR CREATE SPACE

YOUR CREATE SPACE

MONTH AT A GLANCE

Plug your tasks, key dates and projects for the month into the overview. Are you doing a sprint? Block it off in the calendar.

MONDAY	TUESDAY	WEDNESDAY	THURSDAY

FRIDAY	SATURDAY	SUNDAY

REMINDERS / NOTES

YOUR CEO / VISION SPACE

REVIEW YOUR MONTH

	THIS MONTH	LAST MONTH	+/- CHANGE
EMAIL SUBSCRIBERS			
PAGEVIEWS			
BOUNCE RATE			
5 MOST POPULAR POSTS (IN GOOGLE ANALYTICS)			
AVERAGE SESSION TIME			
TOP 5 TRAFFIC REFERRERS			

Track each of your emails sent out this month.

SUBJECT LINE	OPEN RATE	CLICK RATE

EXPENSES	AMOUNT
TOTAL	

REVENUE SOURCE	AMOUNT
TOTAL	

	THIS MONTH	LAST MONTH	+/- CHANGE
Facebook			
Twitter			
Instagram			
LinkedIn			
Pinterest			
YouTube			

CAMPAIGN ANALYSIS

What do you need to take note of the next time you run this same campaign?

What ideas do you have for future content pieces? (Explore the questions that your audience raised during the campaign.)

What can you do to achieve better results?

How much revenue did your campaign earn (if applicable)?

Did you meet your sales target (if applicable)? YES NO

How did it compare to previous campaigns you ran (if applicable)?

If you didn't meet your revenue target, try to pinpoint why this was so (if applicable). For example, maybe you didn't have enough people going through your campaign to meet the goal? Or your sales page didn't convert, although you had a healthy click-through rate?

The following will give you clues:

• High impressions, but low conversions

• High open rate, but low click-through rate

LET'S PLAN MONTH

What's your campaign or theme for the month?

List 3 things you hope to achieve by the end of the month:

GOAL 1

LIST EVERY TASK YOU CAN THINK OF TO COMPLETE YOUR GOAL

GOAL 2

LIST EVERY TASK YOU CAN THINK OF TO COMPLETE YOUR GOAL

GOAL 3

LIST EVERY TASK YOU CAN THINK OF TO COMPLETE YOUR GOAL

CAMPAIGN ONE-SHEET

GOAL OF THE CAMPAIGN

WHAT CONTENT WILL SUPPORT THIS CAMPAIGN AND HELP IT REACH ITS GOALS?

What marketing assets do you need for this campaign? List down everything you can think of. Put a check mark against assets you can reuse.

BLOG POSTS	VIDEOS	LANDING PAGES	EMAILS	SOCIAL MEDIA IMAGES	OTHERS
○	○	○	○	○	○
○	○	○	○	○	○
○	○	○	○	○	○
○	○	○	○	○	○
○	○	○	○	○	○
○	○	○	○	○	○

WHAT DO YOU NEED TO DO TO ATTRACT PEOPLE TO THIS CAMPAIGN?

LIST ALL MAINTENANCE TASKS FOR THE MONTH

LIST ALL MARKETING TASKS FOR THE MONTH

LIST ALL PROJECT TASKS FOR THE MONTH

LIST IMPORTANT DATES FOR THE MONTH

What content will support your goals and/or campaign for this month? Use your campaign one-sheet for guidance. Include any audios, videos and images that you may be repurposing your content into the table as well.

DEADLINE	TITLE

FORMAT	GOAL OF CONTENT / CALL TO ACTION	CONTENT UPGRADE	OUTLINE	DRAFT	EDIT	PUBLISH	REPURPOSE
			○	○	○	○	○
			○	○	○	○	○
			○	○	○	○	○
			○	○	○	○	○
			○	○	○	○	○
			○	○	○	○	○
			○	○	○	○	○
			○	○	○	○	○
			○	○	○	○	○
			○	○	○	○	○
			○	○	○	○	○
			○	○	○	○	○
			○	○	○	○	○
			○	○	○	○	○
			○	○	○	○	○
			○	○	○	○	○
			○	○	○	○	○
			○	○	○	○	○
			○	○	○	○	○

What email content will support your goals and/or campaign for this month? Use your Campaign One-Sheet for guidance. Brainstorm at least 3 subject lines for each email.

GIST OF EMAIL CONTENT	SUBJECT LINE(S)

GOAL/CALL TO ACTION IN EMAIL	SEND DATE	OUTLINE	DRAFT	EDIT	SCHEDULE
		◯	◯	◯	◯
		◯	◯	◯	◯
		◯	◯	◯	◯
		◯	◯	◯	◯
		◯	◯	◯	◯
		◯	◯	◯	◯
		◯	◯	◯	◯
		◯	◯	◯	◯
		◯	◯	◯	◯
		◯	◯	◯	◯
		◯	◯	◯	◯

YOUR CREATE SPACE

YOUR CREATE SPACE

MONTH AT A GLANCE

Plug your tasks, key dates and projects for the month into the overview. Are you doing a sprint? Block it off in the calendar.

MONDAY	TUESDAY	WEDNESDAY	THURSDAY

FRIDAY	SATURDAY	SUNDAY

REMINDERS / NOTES

YOUR CEO / VISION SPACE

REVIEW YOUR MONTH

	THIS MONTH	LAST MONTH	+/- CHANGE
EMAIL SUBSCRIBERS			
PAGEVIEWS			
BOUNCE RATE			
5 MOST POPULAR POSTS (IN GOOGLE ANALYTICS)			
AVERAGE SESSION TIME			
TOP 5 TRAFFIC REFERRERS			

Track each of your emails sent out this month.

SUBJECT LINE	OPEN RATE	CLICK RATE

EXPENSES	AMOUNT
TOTAL	

REVENUE SOURCE	AMOUNT
TOTAL	

	THIS MONTH	LAST MONTH	+/- CHANGE
Facebook			
Twitter			
Instagram			
LinkedIn			
Pinterest			
YouTube			

CAMPAIGN ANALYSIS

What do you need to take note of the next time you run this same campaign?

What ideas do you have for future content pieces? (Explore the questions that your audience raised during the campaign.)

What can you do to achieve better results?

How much revenue did your campaign earn (if applicable)?

Did you meet your sales target (if applicable)?   YES   NO

How did it compare to previous campaigns you ran (if applicable)?

If you didn't meet your revenue target, try to pinpoint why this was so (if applicable). For example, maybe you didn't have enough people going through your campaign to meet the goal? Or your sales page didn't convert, although you had a healthy click-through rate?

The following will give you clues:

• High impressions, but low conversions

• High open rate, but low click-through rate

LET'S PLAN MONTH

What's your campaign or theme for the month?

List 3 things you hope to achieve by the end of the month:

GOAL 1

LIST EVERY TASK YOU CAN THINK OF TO COMPLETE YOUR GOAL

GOAL 2

LIST EVERY TASK YOU CAN THINK OF TO COMPLETE YOUR GOAL

GOAL 3

LIST EVERY TASK YOU CAN THINK OF TO COMPLETE YOUR GOAL

CAMPAIGN ONE-SHEET

GOAL OF THE CAMPAIGN

WHAT CONTENT WILL SUPPORT THIS CAMPAIGN AND HELP IT REACH ITS GOALS?

What marketing assets do you need for this campaign? List down everything you can think of. Put a check mark against assets you can reuse.

BLOG POSTS	VIDEOS	LANDING PAGES	EMAILS	SOCIAL MEDIA IMAGES	OTHERS
◯	◯	◯	◯	◯	◯
◯	◯	◯	◯	◯	◯
◯	◯	◯	◯	◯	◯
◯	◯	◯	◯	◯	◯
◯	◯	◯	◯	◯	◯
◯	◯	◯	◯	◯	◯

WHAT DO YOU NEED TO DO TO ATTRACT PEOPLE TO THIS CAMPAIGN?

LIST ALL MAINTENANCE TASKS FOR THE MONTH

LIST ALL MARKETING TASKS FOR THE MONTH

LIST ALL PROJECT TASKS FOR THE MONTH

LIST IMPORTANT DATES FOR THE MONTH

What content will support your goals and/or campaign for this month? Use your campaign one-sheet for guidance. Include any audios, videos and images that you may be repurposing your content into the table as well.

DEADLINE	TITLE

FORMAT	GOAL OF CONTENT / CALL TO ACTION	CONTENT UPGRADE	OUTLINE	DRAFT	EDIT	PUBLISH	REPURPOSE
			○	○	○	○	○
			○	○	○	○	○
			○	○	○	○	○
			○	○	○	○	○
			○	○	○	○	○
			○	○	○	○	○
			○	○	○	○	○
			○	○	○	○	○
			○	○	○	○	○
			○	○	○	○	○
			○	○	○	○	○
			○	○	○	○	○
			○	○	○	○	○
			○	○	○	○	○
			○	○	○	○	○
			○	○	○	○	○
			○	○	○	○	○
			○	○	○	○	○
			○	○	○	○	○

What email content will support your goals and/or campaign for this month? Use your Campaign One-Sheet for guidance. Brainstorm at least 3 subject lines for each email.

GIST OF EMAIL CONTENT	SUBJECT LINE(S)

GOAL/CALL TO ACTION IN EMAIL	SEND DATE	OUTLINE	DRAFT	EDIT	SCHEDULE
		○	○	○	○
		○	○	○	○
		○	○	○	○
		○	○	○	○
		○	○	○	○
		○	○	○	○
		○	○	○	○
		○	○	○	○
		○	○	○	○
		○	○	○	○
		○	○	○	○

YOUR CREATE SPACE

YOUR CREATE SPACE

MONTH AT A GLANCE

Plug your tasks, key dates and projects for the month into the overview. Are you doing a sprint? Block it off in the calendar.

MONDAY	TUESDAY	WEDNESDAY	THURSDAY

FRIDAY	SATURDAY	SUNDAY

YOUR CEO / VISION SPACE

REVIEW YOUR MONTH

	THIS MONTH	LAST MONTH	+/- CHANGE
EMAIL SUBSCRIBERS			
PAGEVIEWS			
BOUNCE RATE			
5 MOST POPULAR POSTS (IN GOOGLE ANALYTICS)			
AVERAGE SESSION TIME			
TOP 5 TRAFFIC REFERRERS			

Track each of your emails sent out this month.

SUBJECT LINE	OPEN RATE	CLICK RATE

EXPENSES	AMOUNT
TOTAL	

REVENUE SOURCE	AMOUNT
TOTAL	

	THIS MONTH	LAST MONTH	+/- CHANGE
Facebook			
Twitter			
Instagram			
LinkedIn			
Pinterest			
YouTube			

CAMPAIGN ANALYSIS

What do you need to take note of the next time you run this same campaign?

What ideas do you have for future content pieces? (Explore the questions that your audience raised during the campaign.)

What can you do to achieve better results?

How much revenue did your campaign earn (if applicable)?

Did you meet your sales target (if applicable)?   YES   NO

How did it compare to previous campaigns you ran (if applicable)?

If you didn't meet your revenue target, try to pinpoint why this was so (if applicable). For example, maybe you didn't have enough people going through your campaign to meet the goal? Or your sales page didn't convert, although you had a healthy click-through rate?

The following will give you clues:

• High impressions, but low conversions

• High open rate, but low click-through rate

REVIEW
YOUR QUARTER

04

What worked well for you this quarter? (E.g., content that received a lot of comments? A spike in email subscribers?)

How can you replicate these results?

What obstacles are you facing in achieving your goals? Why is it difficult?

Did this quarter help you get closer to your annual objectives?

What can you try to overcome them?

Track the content you published this quarter. How well did it do on your most important social media platform? Track the number of opt-ins each content upgrade received.

CONTENT	SOCIAL SHARES	SIGN-UPS / OPT-INS	COMMENTS

LIST YOUR TOP 5 SUBJECT LINES FOR THIS QUARTER			
SUBJECT LINE	OPEN RATE	CLICK RATE	SUBSCRIBER ENGAGEMENT

LIST YOUR TOP 5 MOST POPULAR CONTENT UPGRADES FOR THIS QUARTER	SUBSCRIBERS

LET'S REVIEW YOUR CONTENT STRATEGY FOR THE QUARTER

Do you see any patterns in the type of content that attract an audience to your site? What can you learn about the type of content people want to read from you?

How can you capitalize on the success of these content pieces? (Examples: Add content upgrades, develop a related product, create similar content, repurpose existing content.)

LET'S REVIEW YOUR EMAIL STRATEGY FOR THE QUARTER

Do you see any patterns in the type of subject lines that worked well for your list? (Examples: Showing a result, using odd and specific numbers, highlighting benefits, expressing curiosity, showing your personal side, raising a question.)

Which emails received the most engagement and replies from your list? Can you tell why?

What opt-in incentive/landing page is working in terms of conversion rate? Keep it status quo or change it up?

Do you need to clean your list? (Re-engage or delete subscribers who haven't opened or clicked on your emails in 3 months or more.)

Do you need to make changes to how your website is optimized? (E.g., Are there any posts with lots of traffic but not converting to subscribers? Do you need to add extra opt-in forms? Do you need to add testimonials to a landing page?)

Are there any emails with a high unsubscribe rate? Can you tell why?

Do you see any patterns in the type of content upgrades that get the most opt-ins?

Where did most subscribers come from?

BECAUSE TO FOLLOW A CALLING REQUIRES WORK. IT'S HARD. IT HURTS. IT DEMANDS ENTERING THE PAIN-ZONE OF EFFORT, RISK, AND EXPOSURE.

STEVEN PRESSFIELD, *TURNING PRO*

YOU MADE IT TO THE END!

Building a blog and business is challenging.

It takes courage to chase your dreams and determination to show up every single day. It won't be easy, but your work *will* inspire and touch others.

When you feel yourself deviating from your goals, slipping into your old routines, or feeling overwhelmed, keep your "why" front and center. Take it one task a day and you'll be much further along in a month than if you never started. Focus on your journey and stop comparing it to someone else's middle.

Before you go, remember to download your bonuses at **CREATEPLANNER.COM/PLANNER-BONUS/**.

If you want to get in touch, come find me here at my slice of the internet: www.meerakothand.com.

I can't wait to see what you create, and I'm rooting for you! Tag me @meerakothand with a picture of this planner as you're working through it.

Good luck and thank you for sharing your work with the world!

Meera

STAY CONNECTED

🌐
MEERAKOTHAND.COM

📷
@MEERAKOTHAND

▶️
/MEERAKOTHAND

f
/MEERAKOTHAND

✉️
MEERA@MEERAKOTHAND.COM

ABOUT THE AUTHOR
MEERA KOTHAND

Meera's an author and speaker who specializes in making marketing for your online business ridiculously simple. She's got seven books on the Amazon Best-Sellers list including *The One Hour Content Plan* and *The Blog Startup*. She's also the founder of the popular CREATE planners and MeeraKothand. Com, an award-winning site listed as one of the top 100 Sites for Solopreneurs three years in a row. Over the years she has developed a reputation for making the most complex topics simple and smashing misconceptions about what you HAVE to do in order to be successful in business.

Through her best-selling books and marketing courses, Meera has taught over 80,000 students and readers, giving them the confidence to build a community that's obsessed with everything they offer.

NEXT STEPS

The ADDICTED Business Academy

What if you had a tested online success road map and the power to create products and launches that fly. What if you were also armed with a system to tie content & profit together. Working on your business doesn't have to feel terrifying or exhausting anymore. If you're looking for training, support, and access to me, you will love The ADDICTED Business Academy. In the academy, I share the actual step-by-step strategies and tactics I've used to build repeat customers and a six-figure business.

Profitable Email System™

What if you could grow a targeted list of subscribers that are primed to buy your product, increase your expert status just by writing mind reading sequences, and say goodbye to emails that get only a fraction of the opens, replies, and clicks they should get? The Profitable Email System is the A–Z email program that shows you EXACTLY how to turn email into an automated sales and list building machine for your blog or business.

Product in 7

What if you could create a digital product in days instead of months? But not just any digital product...one that sells effortlessly? Product in 7 will give you the best hacks and strategies to minimize the amount of time it takes to create your first (or next) product! It bakes a lot of marketing into the process so that you don't ever have to worry about not making a single sale. Create your first or next tiny product with this shockingly simple, templatized product creation process.

Shop the entire suite of courses, books, tools and more at
meerakothand.com/shop-now/

RESOURCES

1. NewsCred, "50 Stats You Need to Know about Content Marketing," Slideshare, June 14, 2013, https://www.slideshare.net/NewsCred/50-best-stats-presentation.

2. Pamela Bump, "31 Business Blogging Stats You Need to Know in 2021," HubSpot (blog), May 11, 2020, https://blog.hubspot.com/marketing/business-blogging-in-2015.

3. Matthew Collis, "Why You Shouldn't Underestimate Email Marketing: Statistics," The American Genius, November 14, 2012, https://theamericangenius.com/business-marketing/why-you-shouldnt-underestimate-the-value-of-email-marketing/.

4. 70 Email Marketing Stats Every Marketer Should Know," Campaign Monitor, December 18, 2018, https://www.campaignmonitor.com/blo...d-to-know/.

Made in the USA
Monee, IL
20 October 2021